Amazing Facts
about Australian
Mammals

Text by Pat Slater

Steve Parish
DISCOVER & LEARN
ABOUT AUSTRALIA

www.steveparish.com.au

Contents

THE PLACENTAL MAMMALS

MAKING MORE DISCOVERIES

Australia's fascinating mammals

The termite-eating Numbat survives only in small areas of forest in southwest WA

There is no need to write fiction about Australia's remarkable mammals. The facts about them are amazing enough.

The distant ancestors of Australian mammals lived when our land was part of the giant super-continent Gondwana. Much of it was covered by rainforest. Shifts in the Earth's surface moved Australia slowly northwards, away from other land masses and eventually the continent became much drier. Some mammals remained in the shrinking rainforests, while others changed so they could survive in the new, more arid landscapes. The eventual arrival of humans changed the existence of Australia's mammals in many ways.

This book gives an overview of today's Australian mammals.

The Bottlenosed Dolphin is found in many places around Australia's coasts

The Dugong is the Australian representative of a group which is becoming rare worldwide

About this book

The Index inside the back cover of this book will give ready reference to the mammals illustrated in its pages. The text and the FACTS columns give information about the animals pictured, about their place in the animal world and about their relatives.

The Glossary on page 79 explains words marked with an asterisk (*) in the text. Some further reading is listed on page 80 but you may wish to visit your local library to consult other references books. A map on the same page shows locations referred to in the text.

Welcome to the wonderful world of Australia's mammals!

The Common Brushtail Possum can live in bush or city

These Euros can exist successfully in arid areas

What is a mammal?

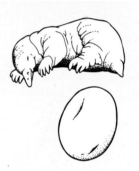

A mammal is an animal which has a backbone and whose well-developed brain is protected by a skull. Its heart has four chambers which separate fresh from used blood. Using the heat generated in its body, a mammal keeps its internal temperature much the same no matter what the temperature of its surroundings. The hair which grows from a mammal's skin acts as insulation to help this. All mammals have mammary glands*, which in female mammals develop so that they can feed their young ones on milk. Mammals have four limbs, which may be adapted for swimming or, in bats, for flight.

Common Sheathtail Bat

Koala

The three different sorts of mammal are separated on the ways they produce young

Echidnas are monotremes

MONOTREMES* lay soft-shelled eggs. The tiny young which hatches from a monotreme egg is naked, blind and has undeveloped hindlimbs. It uses its forelimbs to drag itself to its mother's belly, where it suckles on a patch where milk oozes onto the skin. The Short-beaked Echidna has a pouch, the Platypus does not.

Echidna egg and young one

Kangaroos are marsupials

MARSUPIALS* give birth to tiny young which are naked, blind and have undeveloped hindlimbs. The baby uses its forelimbs to drag itself to one of its mother's nipples, where it attaches itself. Here, it suckles milk and completes its development. It may be protected by a pouch, or by folds of skin.

Kangaroo joey attached to nipple in pouch

Flying-foxes are placental mammals

PLACENTAL MAMMALS* keep their young ones inside their bodies until they are well-developed. This is possible because a placenta* links the blood vessels of mother and baby and prevents the mother's body from rejecting the baby. Once born, the baby suckles milk from its mother's nipples when it is hungry.

Flying-fox young one clinging to its mother

To which group do Australian mammals belong?

Monotremes	Marsupials	Placental Mammals
PLATYPUS ECHIDNA	DASYURIDS* BANDICOOTS AND BILBIES MARSUPIAL MOLE, NUMBAT WOMBATS AND KOALA POSSUMS AND RELATIVES KANGAROOS AND RELATIVES	FLYING-FOXES AND INSECTIVOROUS* BATS RODENTS SEALS AND SEA-LION WHALES AND DOLPHINS DUGONG

The rare Greater Bilby has suffered from competition by rabbits and stock, and predation by foxes and cats

The intruders

Humans have introduced many placental mammals to Australia.

The Dingo came with seafarers from southeast Asia. The House Mouse and two rat species stowed away on the First Fleet in 1788. Europeans deliberately introduced cats, dogs, rabbits, hares, foxes, horses, donkeys, pigs, camels, sheep, cattle, water buffalo and goats, as pets, food animals or working animals, or for sport. Some domestic animals, like cats and dogs, have become feral* and, like foxes, prey on native* Australian animals. Some introduced mammals, like rabbits, compete with them for food and shelter. Others, like sheep, goats, cattle, buffalo and pigs, change their habitat.

The feral cat preys on native animals

FACTS

▶ Australia's largest marsupial, the male Red Kangaroo, may weigh 85 kg. It may measure 2.4 m from nosetip to tailtip, with a tail 1 m long.

▶ Australia's smallest marsupial, the Long-tailed Planigale, weighs only 4 g and measures 12 cm from nosetip to tailtip, with a tail 6 cm long.

▶ Some of Australia's mammals such as the Koala, Platypus and Numbat rely on one special food or habitat for survival.

▶ If their special food or shelter disappears, or a major predator* or disease appears, animals like these will become extinct. Once reduced beyond a certain number, they cannot breed up again.

7

The different sorts of mammals

The Common Wombat (*Vombatus ursinus*)

Scientific and common names

Every animal is known by two sorts of names.

The **scientific name**, which is made from Latin or Greek words, remains the same all over the world. The first word of a scientific name places the animal in a **genus** with other animals closely related to it. The second word is the animal's **species**.

Animals of the same species can breed with each other and produce fertile offspring.

So the Common Wombat's generic name is *Vombatus* (wombat). Its specific name is *ursinus* (bear-like). Even if two zoologists did not speak a common language, if one of them said "*Vombatus ursinus*" the other one would know exactly which mammal was being referred to.

The **common name** varies from country to country according to the language spoken. The common name of a species uses capital letters, e.g. Common Wombat, Red Kangaroo or Striped Possum. However, the common name of a group of animals, such as wombats, kangaroos or possums, takes a lower-case letter.

Two-tooths and many-tooths

Zoologists divide all marsupials into two groups based on their lower incisors

Two lower incisors (diprotodonts*)	More than two lower incisors (polyprotodonts*)
KOALA - eats leaves WOMBATS - eat shrubs and grass POSSUMS - eat leaves, nectar, fruit, sap and insects KANGAROOS - eat shrubs and grass	DASYURIDS - eat animals of all types and sizes BANDICOOTS - eat invertebrate* animals and fungi MARSUPIAL MOLE - eats burrowing insects NUMBAT - eats insects (termites)

BANDICOOT UPPER AND LOWER JAWS
incisors nip; canines stab; premolars shear; molars grind

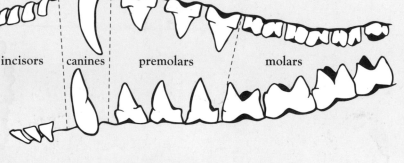

incisors   canines   premolars   molars

Northern Bandicoot is classed as a polyprotodont

IAN MORRIS

How mammals have developed through the ages

MONOTREMES · **MARSUPIALS** · **PLACENTALS**

Tasmania cut off

Humans arrive, megafauna becomes extinct

Present

QUATERNARY

2 million years ago

Australia's mammal species respond to more arid climatic conditions

TERTIARY

Australia separates from Antarctica and begins to drift northwards

65 million years ago

Dinosaurs and flying reptiles become extinct

Marsupials and placentals diverge

CRETACEOUS

145 million years ago

Reptiles, including dinosaurs and flying pterosaurs, dominant on earth

First birds appear

Monotremes diverge from other mammals

JURASSIC

True mammals appear

208 million years ago

Mammal-like reptiles appear

TRIASSIC

Reptiles, including dinosaurs, dominate land

245 million years ago

Amphibians decline in numbers, reptiles become more abundant

PERMIAN

The history of Australia's mammals

The first inhabitants

An opalised platypus jaw found at Lightning Ridge has been dated to around 120 million years before the present. At that time, Australia was part of the super-continent Gondwana. By 60 to 50 million years ago, Australia had separated from Antarctica and begun to move northwards, carrying mammals which would survive after most of the relatives they left behind in other land masses died out.

For many millions of years most of Australia remained covered by rainforests. Around 15 million years ago, the continent became drier and gradually most of the rainforests were replaced by eucalypts, acacias and other plants suited to dry conditions. Some mammals remained in the rainforests. Others, such as the Koala, adapted their lifestyles and diets to survive in the new habitats.

Twenty-five million years ago, koala-like animals lived in rainforests. Today's Koala eats eucalypts

The recent arrivals

Though marsupials were the dominant group of mammals when Australia began its "voyage", recent fossil discoveries indicate that there were some placentals present. Around 20 million years ago, a new group of placentals, the bats, flew in. New rodent species drifted to shore on floating debris as Australia neared Asia about five million years ago. Aboriginal ancestors arrived more than 60 000 years ago. The hunting and burning practices of their descendants may have affected the huge animals known as the megafauna, most of which had disappeared by 20 000 years ago. The Dingo was probably brought to Australia by southeast Asian seafarers between 4000 and 3000 years ago. An efficient predator, it displaced the marsupial "tiger", the Thylacine, from the mainland. Europeans settled in 1788. Their activities and the animals they introduced have greatly affected all of Australia's native mammals and caused the extinction of some.

The Mountain Pygmy-possum was known only from fossil material until a living specimen was found in 1966

The Dingo was brought to Australia less than 4000 years ago

Finding out from fossils

Fossils are the traces of animals or plants which lived at some time in the past.

A fossil may be an organism which has been preserved whole, as an insect is preserved in the fossilised tree sap we call amber. A fossil may be an imprint, such as a footprint, made in mud but preserved when the mud changed into stone. It may be a stone cast, produced when flesh, bone or plant material was replaced by rock. Some fossils can be dated by measuring the degree to which radioactive* substances in them or around them have decayed since they were formed.

Skulls and teeth are amongst the commoner fossil finds

HOW A FOSSIL IS FORMED

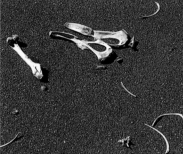

A kangaroo dies ...   its bones are covered by soil ...   and gradually replaced by stone

MEGAFAUNA!

As recently as 30 000 years ago, and perhaps as recently as 6000 years ago, Australia was home to a group of very large animals, the megafauna.

These giants included a leaf-eating kangaroo, *Procoptodon*, which stood three metres high, a flesh-eating marsupial "lion", *Thylacoleo*, and a giant wombat called *Phascolonus*. The largest marsupial which ever lived, the rhinoceros-sized, wombat-like *Diprotodon*, may have survived until 6000 years ago. There are two main theories to account for the mass extinction of the megafauna. Perhaps climatic change led to long and severe drought. Human burning of large tracts of country over centuries may have altered the vegetation. Perhaps hunting took its toll of the giants as well.

The *Diprotodon* was a giant herbivorous marsupial

FACTS

▶ People who study fossils are called palaeontologists.

▶ Fossil evidence of Australia's ancient mammals has been gathered from sites such as Riversleigh (Qld), Alcoota (NT), Naracoorte (SA), Wellington Caves (NSW), Dinosaur Cove (Vic) and Devils Lair (WA).

▶ Fossils embedded in limestone, as they are at Riversleigh, are retrieved by dissolving the limestone in a 10% solution of acetic acid, which does not dissolve bone.

▶ Sometimes rock must be removed from around fossils with chisels, small picks and dental drills.

These baby Northern Quolls will watch how their mother finds food

WADE HUGHES

Acting on information received

A mammal learns about its surroundings by using its eyes to see, its ears to hear, its nose to smell, its tongue to taste and its skin to feel.

The information received interacts in the animal's brain with signals from inside its body. Then the mammal acts in a way that makes it feel better or avoids danger. For example, if a kangaroo feels hungry, it sights, smells and tastes grass, then eats it. If it sees or smells a predator such as a Dingo, it hops away.

Behaviour is the name given to all the actions carried out by an animal.

Instinctive behaviour is carried out by all similar animals in the same situation. Any Koala will instinctively climb a tree to escape danger.

Learned behaviour is carried out because the animal is copying another animal's actions, or because it has discovered by trial and error that the action succeeds. A young quoll will learn to hunt from watching its mother hunt, and to attack prey from playing with its litter-mates.

Mammals can overcome instinctive reactions in order to survive. A wallaby may learn to come close to humans where it is fed regularly, though it may remain wary elsewhere.

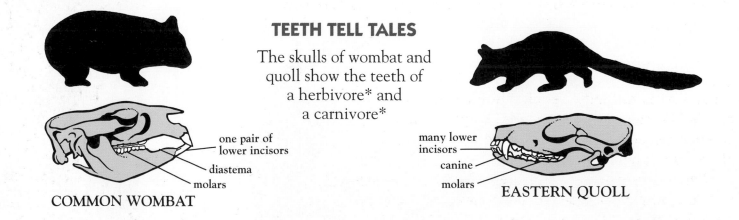

TEETH TELL TALES

The skulls of wombat and quoll show the teeth of a herbivore* and a carnivore*

one pair of lower incisors

diastema

molars

COMMON WOMBAT

many lower incisors

canine

molars

EASTERN QUOLL

A mammal's teeth reveal many facts about the owner's diet and way of getting food.

Herbivores like wombats and kangaroos have sharp incisors which nip or tear off plants, then a bare space called a diastema* which allows the tongue to push a wad of plants back to the grinding molars. Omnivores* like bandicoots have a mixture of teeth types which can deal with both animal and plant food.

Large carnivores like the Dingo have dagger-like canine teeth which stab and hold prey, shearing premolars which cut off pieces of flesh, and strong molars which crush bones. Small carnivores such as dunnarts have stiletto-like canines, which can pierce the tough outer skeletons of insects, centipedes and scorpions.

Where Australia's animals find their food

In the trees - Spotted Cuscus

In the air - Orange Horseshoe-bat

On the ground - Bennett's Wallaby

In the water - Australian Fur-seal

Animals with central heating

A mammal is an endothermic* animal, whose body is "heated from inside" and stays much the same temperature, no matter how hot or cold the surroundings.

When a mammal's body breaks down food and oxygen in order to build new tissue and to supply energy, heat is produced. Hair, which grows out of the mammal's skin, and fat, which lies under it, help insulate the mammal's body against heat loss.

If the mammal becomes too hot, it cools itself by sleeking down its hair, sweating, panting or moving to a cool place. If the mammal becomes too cold, goosebumps pull its hair erect, it shivers to make extra body heat, and moves to a warmer place.

As a Dingo pants, saliva evaporates, cooling the blood flowing through the tongue and roof of the mouth

13

FACTS
ABOUT HOT BODIES

▶ Monotremes have a normal body temperature of 30°C. Marsupials average 35°C, while human body temperature is normally 37°C.

▶ Mammals have four-chambered hearts, which efficiently pump heat-carrying blood around their bodies.

▶ In hot conditions, a mammal's surface blood vessels expand and radiate heat. In cold, the surface blood vessels constrict, retaining body heat.

▶ Desert mammals often have big ears and rangy bodies. The large skin area loses heat fast.

▶ Mammals which live in cold places have compact bodies and thick fur. Insulating fat beneath their skins can be used by the body as a food source in very cold weather.

▶ The bodies of small mammals need to "burn" food and oxygen at a high level in order to maintain their body temperatures.

▶ Some animals, like small bats and echidnas, survive cold by going into a short-term resting state called torpor*, or a longer "sleep" called hibernation*.

Duck-billed wonder

PETER MARSACK

The Platypus is a monotreme, "an animal with one hole". Like the other monotreme, the echidna, and reptiles and birds, it has one vent, called the cloaca*, through which digestive wastes, urine, eggs and sperm all leave its body.

This remarkable mammal lives near unpolluted waterways in eastern Australia, from Cooktown south to Tasmania. It spends much of its time in the water and its eyes are set on top of its head, while its nostrils open on top of the leathery bill. The fine, dense fur is waterproof.

A Platypus hunts underwater for small aquatic animals such as insect larvae, shrimps and worms. These are stored in cheek pouches, then taken to the surface, where they are chewed between horny grinding plates and ridges on the Platypus's upper and lower jaws, then swallowed. (A baby Platypus has teeth, but loses them about the time that it is weaned.)

The broad, flat tail of the Platypus is used to store body fat.

When the Platypus walks, the webs of the front feet are turned back so the claws contact the ground

PETER MARSACK

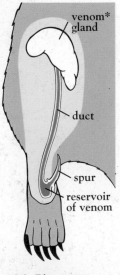

The improbable Platypus

When the first Platypus skin arrived in England about 200 years ago, scientists thought it was a fake. They could not imagine any animal with a wide, leathery bill, a furry body, a broad tail and webbed feet. They thought it impossible that a female mammal should lay eggs, or that a male mammal should have venomous spurs on its ankles.

When the scientists finally accepted the Platypus as a real animal, they called it *Ornithorhynchus anatinus*, meaning "duck-like bird-snout".

Amongst modern discoveries about the Platypus is the fact that it swims with its eyes, ears and nostrils shut. It locates the small water animals on which it feeds by detecting electric signals from their bodies with special sensors on its wide, flat bill.

A Platypus propels itself with its forefeet, using its hindfeet as brakes and for steering. It may stay submerged for up to one minute.

A Platypus paddling at the surface of the water

The lower edge of the bill shields the throat

In the water, the webs of the front feet form paddles

FACTS ABOUT PLATYPUS FOSSILS

▶ An opalised Platypus jawbone from Lightning Ridge is around 120 million years old.

▶ In 1991 and 1992, three fossil Platypus teeth were found in Argentinian Patagonia. Their owner lived between 63 and 61 million years ago. At that time, the region was probably linked to Australia via Antarctica.

▶ Fossil Platypus teeth 25 million years old have been found in South Australia. A fossil Platypus skull, including teeth, 15 million years old was found at Riversleigh, Qld.

Eggs in a burrow

The spurs of the male Platypus are probably used in territorial fights in the springtime breeding season. Mating takes place in the water. The female digs a breeding burrow which may be up to 20 metres in length. She lays two soft, sticky eggs, each about 17 millimetres long, then incubates* them between her abdomen and tail for about two weeks. The young suck milk that oozes onto patches on her abdomen. They leave the burrow after three months and are weaned at between four and five months.

Water does not penetrate the dense fur of the Platypus

Ant-eater with spines

The Short-beaked Echidna, like the Platypus, is a monotreme, whose young is hatched from an egg. Found all over Australia, the Short-beaked Echidna is covered with sharp spines and has strong legs and claws.

When threatened, the echidna either rolls into a spiky ball or digs down into the ground. The echidna feeds on ants and termites and its mouth and nostrils are on the end of a long, sensitive snout kept moist with mucus. It opens up termite or ant nests with claws and snout, pokes in its saliva-covered tongue and flicks insects back into its mouth.

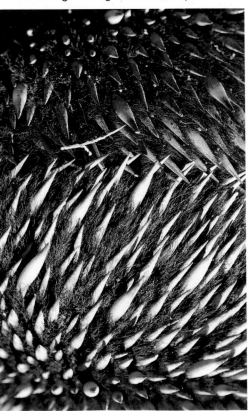

The two long claws on the Short-beaked Echidna's hindfoot are used for grooming between its spines

On soft ground, an echidna can dig rapidly downwards

On hard ground, a threatened echidna rolls into a ball

Fur grows between the echidna's sharp spines

DID YOU KNOW?

FACTS

▶ There are only three monotreme species, the Platypus, the Short-beaked Echidna of Australia and the much larger Long-beaked Echidna of New Guinea.

▶ The Short-beaked Echidna's scientific name, *Tachyglossus aculeatus*, means "spiny fast-tongue".

▶ An echidna can lift objects twice its own weight.

▶ The record lifespan for a captive echidna is 49 years.

▶ Sometimes an echidna lies on an ant-mound, sticks out its tongue and lets ants walk onto it. Eventually, it pulls back its tongue and swallows the ants.

▶ Termites, an echidna's main food, contain up to 77% water, but echidnas are sometimes seen drinking. Echidnas can swim.

JIRI LOCHMAN

An echidna drinking

The Short-beaked Echidna has broad paws with strong claws. Mucus keeps the sensitive end of its snout moist

Making more echidnas

Echidnas mate between June and September. Up to eight males may form a "train" which follows a female around for up to four weeks. The males push and shove each other and the male who is the most persistent eventually breeds with the female. Mating takes place belly-to-belly, which avoids the male spiking himself on the female's spines.

About 14 days after mating, the female lays a leathery-shelled egg, which is incubated in her pouch for about ten days before hatching into a baby which sucks milk from a patch on its mother's belly. The tiny baby cannot store iron in its body and the large amount of haemoglobin, an iron-carrying substance, in the mother's milk colours the fluid pink. The milk is very weak when the baby first suckles, but by the time it is weaned the milk is nearly 50 per cent solids.

The young one stays in the pouch until its spikes develop, then it is left in a nursery burrow. The mother returns to suckle the baby every five to ten days and the young echidna takes in around 20 per cent of its body weight in milk at each feed. It is very vulnerable to predators during this stage of its life. The young echidna leaves the burrow between six and eight weeks after hatching.

ECHIDNA SNOUT

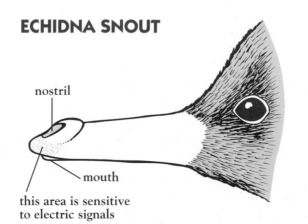

nostril

mouth

this area is sensitive
to electric signals

Fierce little hunters

Many carnivorous marsupials have crests or brushes on their tails. They are called dasyurids, meaning "hairy-tailed animals". They include the mouse-sized dunnarts, the large-rat-sized phascogales, the cat-sized quolls and the dog-sized Tasmanian Devil, the largest living dasyurid.

Brush-tailed Phascogale

IAN MORRIS

Australia's smallest mammal (the world's second-smallest) is a dasyurid, the Long-tailed Planigale. The Thylacine (once miscalled the marsupial "tiger" or "wolf"), was also a dasyurid. It is almost certainly extinct.

The dasyurids have many sharp front teeth, which they use for stabbing and holding their prey. Small dasyurids hunt spiders, centipedes, insects, mammals and reptiles. Larger ones eat birds, mammals, reptiles and sometimes carrion.

IAN MORRIS

A female Fawn Antechinus may have 16 babies but has only ten nipples. Some babies will not survive

The male Yellow-footed Antechinus dies after breeding

Common Planigale, one of the world's smallest mammals

Backpacking babies

Females of some dasyurid species have a pouch. Other species have no pouch at all, or just folds of skin over the nipples. When a dasyurid baby is born, it fastens its mouth onto a nipple and stays there until it is too large for its mother to drag around under her belly. It may then ride on her back or be hauled around clinging to its mother's fur. If it falls off, it calls loudly until its mother returns to retrieve it. More mature youngsters may be left in a nest while the mother hunts. She brings back prey for them to share and the young ones practise their hunting skills by playfully stalking and pouncing on each other.

Mate, then die

In August and September each year, males of at least nine species of small dasyurid become obsessed with breeding. Male antechinuses and phascogales spend enormous amounts of energy seeking females and mating with them and fighting other males. The stress is so great that in most species no males survive until their babies are born. Their immune systems collapse, leaving them no protection against disease, and they die. The females give birth, raise young and may live to breed again the following season.

A Kowari, found in Central Australia's stony deserts, eating a gecko

IAN MORRIS

WADE HUGHES

FACTS

▶ Male Brown Antechinuses spend the two-week breeding season mating with females for up to six hours at a time. At the end of the two weeks, only female Brown Antechinuses are left alive. Their litters are all born within a ten-day period.

▶ In 1967, photographer Michael Morcombe set a trap for nectar-eating marsupials on a banksia flower at Cheyne Beach, on the south coast of WA. He caught two Southern Dibblers, a species not recorded for 83 years. The photograph below, taken in 1967, shows one of those animals.

▶ In 1985, another population of Southern Dibblers was found on islands in Jurien Bay, WA. One male was observed to mate with six females in four days. All males died within one week of the breeding season.

Southern Dibbler

M & I MORCOMBE

FACTS

▶ The tiny planigales have wedge-shaped heads, with which they pry into cracks and shovel aside litter while hunting prey. A planigale may eat its own weight in food in one day.

▶ The Red-cheeked Dunnart has a head plus body length of 10.5 cm. Its tail is about 11 cm long. For comparison, the head and body of a large House Mouse can measure up to 9.5 cm and its tail up to 9.0 cm.

▶ Some small dasyurids become torpid if the temperature drops. They must shiver to warm their muscles before they can become active once again.

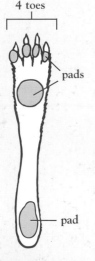

4 toes

pads

pad

The Kultarr has a typical dasyurid foot

Hunters of the aridlands

Some of the small dasyurids are particularly well adapted to life in arid regions. They spend the day in a burrow, a tree hollow or rock crevice, conserving moisture, emerging at dusk to hunt. They obtain fluid from the animals they eat and from licking the dew which forms overnight.

IAN MORRIS

The Red-cheeked Dunnart hunts almost any animal smaller than itself

The Mulgara, which lives in Central Australia, burrows by day and hunts spiders, insects and rodents at night. Its body uses most of the water taken in and the animal excretes very concentrated urine.

The Kultarr is another desert-dweller, which has long hindlegs and a very long, tufted tail. When moving fast it bounds rather than hops, pivoting and changing direction on its forefeet. This may help it avoid counter-strikes by its dangerous prey, which includes venomous centipedes, spiders and scorpions.

JIRI LOCHMAN

This female Mulgara is eating an insect while one young one clings to her back and another watches

The Kultarr of Central Australia has a long, tufted tail. When moving fast, it does not hop but bounds

▸ Early European settlers called quolls "native polecats", or "native cats". The name "quoll" is an Aboriginal word for the Eastern Quoll.

▸ The Western Quoll's Aboriginal name, "Chuditch", echoes the explosive noise the animal makes when threatened.

▸ The largest quoll, the Spotted-tailed, may weigh up to 7 kg. The smallest, the Northern Quoll, may weigh less than 1 kg.

▸ The Northern Quoll may visit campsites and bush homes looking for food. It has declined in numbers in areas of Qld and the NT after the arrival of the introduced, poisonous Cane Toad.

▸ Quolls suffer from competition with feral domestic cats and foxes, which eat the same prey.

▸ A quoll kills its prey by biting the back of the head or neck.

▸ The Spotted-tailed Quoll is the only quoll whose spots extend onto the tail.

A pair of Northern Quolls mating

JIRI LOCHMAN

QUOLLS

Spotted predators

Quolls are medium-sized dasyurids, easily recognised by their white spots. They are nocturnal hunters of birds, small mammals, lizards and insects, but will also scavenge carcasses and eat fruit.

Quolls have disappeared from many areas of Australia as the forests they live in have been cut down or altered. The Northern Quoll, smallest of the four Australian species, lives in woodland and rocky country across northern Australia and is the only quoll still found in much of its former range.

The Eastern Quoll is now found only in Tasmania, the massive Spotted-tailed Quoll lives in eastern coastal forests and the Western Quoll is restricted to the extreme southwest of Western Australia.

The Spotted-tailed Quoll is found in forests from southern Queensland to northern Victoria and Tasmania

IAN MORRIS

A Northern Quoll scavenging a fish carcass hung in a tree

A rare Eastern Quoll ear-tagged for study

FACTS

▶ The female Eastern Quoll may give birth to as many as 30 young ones, but has only six nipples. The babies which cannot attach to a nipple perish.

▶ A newborn quoll is the size of a grain of rice.

▶ When a female quoll becomes pregnant, folds of skin on her abdomen develop into a pouch.

▶ Baby quolls remain attached to their mother's nipples for between eight and ten weeks. By the time they shift to her back, her nipples may be torn and infected.

▶ When young quolls are too large to be carried by their mother while she is hunting, they are left in a nest. She returns to feed them there for around two to three months.

▶ Young quolls tumble and wrestle, stalk each other and chase each other's tails. This play is good practice for later hunting.

This Western Quoll, or Chuditch, is eating a Ringneck Parrot

Island scavenger

Once the Thylacine (see page 26) was eliminated from Tasmania, the next-biggest marsupial carnivore, the Tasmanian Devil, took its place in popular legend as a menace to livestock. The Devil certainly looks fierce and has been known to kill penned poultry and to take lambs. However, it is a scavenger* rather than a hunter and often feeds on the carcasses of animals it finds in the bush or on roads. In spite of its menacing jaws, a Tasmanian Devil is easily killed by a determined dog.

Tasmanian Devils emerge from their dens at night to wander long distances looking for food. Several may gather at a carcass (22 were counted feeding on a dead cow). The Devils growl, gape and yell at each other. They may interlock jaws, but actual injuries are rare. Until 600 years ago, the Tasmanian Devil still existed on mainland Australia, but it is thought that the Dingo took over its place in the environment and today it is found only in Tasmania. The Devil is thought to have increased in numbers in Tasmania during the 200 years of European settlement. There are plenty of road kills to be eaten and farmers' fields provide corbie grubs (these agricultural pests are one of the Devil's favourite foods). Devils may even be seen on the outskirts of Tasmanian towns, presumably checking out the dining possibilities.

A Tasmanian Devil challenges a rival

DID YOU KNOW?

FACTS

▶ A male Tasmanian Devil can weigh between 9 and 12 kg, while a female weighs between 5 and 8 kg.

▶ An Aboriginal man buried around 7000 years ago at Lake Nitchle in western NSW wore a necklace of 178 teeth, which had been taken from at least 47 Tasmanian Devils.

▶ The Tasmanian Devil has very powerful jaws and sharp teeth. Bones are cracked on the second molar tooth, which is a blunt stump by the time the owner is three years old.

▶ A Tasmanian Devil is not a fast runner, rocking along at less than 13 km/h.

▶ The Devil's tracks show one paw print, followed by two side by side, then another single print.

FRONT PAW

HIND PAW

Paw prints of Tasmanian Devil

A mother's life

Tasmanian Devils mate in March and the young are born in April. The female has four nipples and her pouch opens backwards. She will have two young when two years of age, then three or four babies annually for the next three years. Her life expectancy will be seven or eight years.

Tasmanian Devils are active after dark

Playful youngsters

Young Tasmanian Devils are very playful. They wrestle and tumble with each other, biting and chewing and making a lot of noise. Much of the fearsome gaping of jaws could be practice for later competition at mealtimes. Hand-reared young Tasmanian Devils become very tame. "Carers" who bring up young animals orphaned when their mother is killed (often by being hit by a vehicle) describe young Devils as "delightful". Hand-reared youngsters must be released into the wild eventually, so for the animals' own good the carers do not treat them as pets.

A pair of Tasmanian Devils being hand-reared

Young Devils

Young Tasmanian Devils spend 15 weeks in their mother's pouch. When they are too big for the pouch, she will leave them in a nest and return to feed them at intervals. It may be another 15 weeks before they are weaned and towards the end of this time they may follow her around.

Young Tasmanian Devils spend a lot of time in play

FACTS

▶ One Tasmanian Devil may have a territory of up to 20 hectares, but several territories may overlap.

▶ The naked ears of an agitated Tasmanian Devil turn deep red.

▶ Young Tasmanian Devils are much more active than adults and can climb up sloping trunks and into bushes to find roosting birds.

▶ A high proportion of young Tasmanian Devils survive until they are weaned at between seven and eight months of age. After that, the death rate is high.

▶ The maximum age to which a Tasmanian Devil has lived in captivity is eight years.

▶ In 1909 and in 1950, the population of Tasmanian Devils crashed, probably from some disease.

▶ A Tasmanian Devil may store body fat in its short, carrot-shaped tail.

▶ The whiskers on a Devil's face and front legs allow it to feel its way in the dark.

THYLACINE

Gone for ever?

There is always hope that somewhere in the wildest wilds of Tasmania the Thylacine still preys on wallabies. However, the last known wild Thylacine was captured in 1933 and died in 1936.

The forebody of the Thylacine was wolf-like, with jaws which could gape widely. It had strong hindlegs, a long, thick-based tail and the female's pouch opened backwards. Hunting singly or in pairs, it persisted on a trail until it ran down its prey. The Thylacine existed in both New Guinea and Australia and it features in ancient Aboriginal rock art. The Dingo, which occupied the same ecological niche*, was a more efficient predator and by around 2000 years ago the Thylacine was extinct on the mainland. The species continued to exist in Tasmania, which was cut off by the rising sea level from the mainland about 12 000 years ago, before the Dingo arrived in Australia.

This is an artist's impression of the Thylacine. Hopefully the original still exists somewhere in Tasmania

MARSUPIAL MOLE

Blind sand-swimmer

The Marsupial Mole lives in Australia's sandy deserts.

Its eyes are non-functional, its ears are holes surrounded by thick fur. A horny shield protects its snout, its front paws have large digging claws. It eats insects and their larvae and surfaces after rain.

The Marsupial Mole's front and rear limbs have specialised claws

NUMBAT
Striped termite-eater

The Numbat is the only marsupial which feeds exclusively on termites. It is also unusual amongst small marsupials in being active by day. Two hundred years ago, the Numbat was found across Australia. Today, it remains only in a small area of Wandoo eucalypt forest in southwestern Western Australia and is a rare and endangered species.

Baby Numbats cling to their mother's belly

A Numbat locates termites by scent. It lacks the powerful forelimbs needed to open concrete-hard nests, so it claws open the roofs of the shallow runways used by the termites to reach their feeding-places, then licks up the insects with its long, sticky tongue. It has a high energy output and moves fast, tail bristling, scratching at termite trails and licking up the insects so rapidly its tongue is a blur. The female Numbat has four nipples and no pouch. The young are carried clinging to the nipples and the hair around them for some time, then are left in a nest. They may be carried on the mother's back.

FACTS

▶ The Numbat's scientific name, *Myrmecobius fasciatus*, means "striped feeder-on-ants".

▶ A big male Numbat's head and body may be 28 cm long and its tail 21 cm. A male may weigh up to 700 g and a female up to 680 g.

▶ The Numbat's sticky tongue is half as long as its head and body combined.

▶ A Numbat has 52 poorly developed teeth. It uses its mouth to shift small branches and to carry nesting material.

▶ The Numbat shelters in hollow logs. It falls prey to foxes and is vulnerable to fire and other habitat destruction.

▶ Numbats are not wary of vehicles and may be spotted from a car driven slowly along a track through Wandoo forest.

Young Numbats playing at the entrance to their nest in a hollow log

Adult Numbat

Galloping ground-diggers

Eastern Barred Bandicoot

Southern Brown Bandicoot eating

Many people in coastal eastern Australia see small, cone-shaped holes in their lawns and never realise that a bandicoot has been at work, scenting a spider, grub, earthworm or juicy root, then digging it out with strong forepaws and snout. The food is held in the forepaws and crunched noisily.

The hunter may be the Northern Brown Bandicoot (found across northern and eastern coastal Australia south to Sydney), or the Long-nosed Bandicoot, whose range extends right down the east coast. Where these rabbit-sized omnivores feed on road verges, they often fall victim to traffic and they need ground cover for shelter. However, they, and the Southern Brown Bandicoot, seem to be coping with modern life.

Other bandicoots, and their relatives the bilbies, have not been so fortunate. The Pig-footed and Desert Bandicoots and the Lesser Bilby are presumed extinct. The Eastern Barred Bandicoot is restricted to Tasmania and a small area of Victoria. The Western Barred Bandicoot is found only on two islands in Shark Bay, WA, and the Golden Bandicoot also has a limited range. The soft-furred, long-eared Greater Bilby, once common, now exists only in a few desert locations.

The Western Barred Bandicoot is now found only on two small islands in Shark Bay, WA

The Greater Bilby makes a lengthy home burrow

Only one bilby remains

The Greater Bilby lives in dry, hot areas. Destruction of its habitat, competition from rabbits, predation by foxes and disease have contributed to its extreme rarity. Efforts are being made to save this species from the fate of the Lesser Bilby, which is probably extinct.

The Greater Bilby digs a burrow up to three metres in length. It shelters in it by day, emerging to feed on insects, seeds, fruit and fungi at night. Its scientific name, *Macrotis lagotis*, means "hare-eared big-ear" and its large ears with their plentiful blood vessels help its body get rid of heat.

The rare Golden Bandicoot

JIRI LOCHMAN

THE STATUS OF OUR BANDICOOTS AND BILBIES

EXTINCT	ENDANGERED	VULNERABLE	SECURE
		GOLDEN BANDICOOT	
LESSER BILBY		WESTERN BARRED BANDICOOT	LONG-NOSED BANDICOOT
DESERT BANDICOOT		EASTERN BARRED BANDICOOT	NORTHERN BROWN BANDICOOT
PIG-FOOTED BANDICOOT	GREATER BILBY	RUFOUS SPINY BANDICOOT	SOUTHERN BROWN BANDICOOT

(IF HABITAT CHANGES)

FACTS

▶ The Lesser Bilby was last reported alive in 1931, in sandhills in northeast SA. A skull of unknown age was found in 1967, in a Wedge-tailed Eagle's nest located southeast of Alice Springs.

▶ The Golden Bandicoot is now found only on Barrow Island, WA, and in the far northwest Kimberley Division.

▶ Bandicoots have much smaller ears than bilbies. Bandicoots have coarse, water-shedding outer coats of hair and soft fur undercoats. Bilbies have soft fur coats.

▶ Bandicoot or bilby hair comes out in clumps in an attacker's mouth.

▶ A female bandicoot or bilby has eight nipples but seldom rears more than two or three young ones. The pouch opens to the rear.

▶ Bandicoots live on the ground and most build shallow daytime nests.

▶ A bandicoot can leap, but when moving fast it gallops.

Gumleaf gourmet

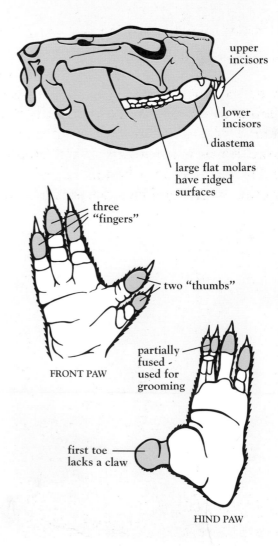

The Koala has long limbs

During the nineteenth and early twentieth centuries, millions of Koalas were killed and their skins exported. The Koala became scarce in some areas, extinct in others. Today, the Koala is a general favourite with Australians and a prime attraction for overseas tourists and energetic efforts are being made to conserve it.

Since the species depends on a limited number of species of eucalypt trees for food, preserving adequate numbers of wild Koalas depends on preserving their habitat.

Fossil evidence shows that Koala ancestors lived in rainforests. However, as Australia became drier, the Koala adapted to eat the leaves of the eucalypt trees which replaced much of the rainforests.

A very restricted diet

A Koala carefully selects a leaf, nips it off, then grinds it up with its molar teeth before swallowing it. The toxic* substances which exist in eucalypt leaves are filtered from the Koala's blood by its liver, and finally are excreted in its urine. Tiny micro-organisms* in the Koala's lengthy caecum* (appendix) ferment the eucalypt leaf fibre and allow the Koala to use the carbohydrates (starches and sugars) it contains. A eucalypt leaf offers 50% water, 18% fibre and supplies only 8% fat, 5% carbohydrates and 4% protein. This diet generates little energy, and once a young Koala is weaned it becomes much less active. The adult Koala eats for around four hours each day and sleeps for just under 20 hours. The remaining one per cent of a Koala's time is used for climbing, changing trees or finding a mate.

Koalas obtain most of their water from leaves and dew, but they may occasionally be seen drinking.

KOALA SKULL AND PAWS

upper incisors

lower incisors

diastema

large flat molars have ridged surfaces

three "fingers"

two "thumbs"

FRONT PAW

partially fused - used for grooming

first toe lacks a claw

HIND PAW

DID YOU KNOW?

FACTS

▸ Male Koalas are up to 50% heavier than females.

▸ Victorian Koalas weigh 8-12 kg. Queensland Koalas weigh 5-7 kg.

▸ Male Koalas live for about ten years, while females can live to 15.

▸ Koalas and wombats probably shared a common ancestor more than 25 million years ago.

▸ The Koala has the largest appendix of any mammal. It is up to 2 m in length.

▸ Koala fur has a high number of hair shafts in a given area of skin compared to other mammals' fur. This makes it waterproof.

▸ If forced to hurry on the ground, a Koala bounds on its long legs with its rump in the air, looking in outline rather like a shorn Old English Sheepdog.

Koala eating leaf

A large Koala cub sits in this position so it can put its head into its mother's pouch to nurse

A Koala grows up

A newborn Koala is bee-sized; it weighs about half a gram and is less than two centimetres long. It stays attached to the nipple for 13 weeks and its eyes open at around 22 weeks. The baby's gut acquires the micro-organisms needed to break down leaves when it eats special droppings called "pap" produced by its mother and its teeth appear when it is about 24 weeks old. It will remain in the pouch for another month and be independent of its mother at about one year of age.

A Koala sleeping in warm weather

A Koala sleeping in cold weather

▶ Koalas are not found only in eucalypts. In one survey, Koalas were seen eating or sitting in nearly 70 species of eucalypts and nearly 30 non-eucalypt species.

▶ In Queensland, the favoured Koala tree is the Forest Red Gum. Victorian Koalas prefer Manna Gum.

▶ The Koala does not occur naturally in Western Australia, nor in the Northern Territory.

▶ In South Australia and Victoria today, wild Koalas are often the descendants of animals brought from overstocked island colonies and released in traditional habitat.

▶ A female Koala can breed at two years of age, a male at five after he has a home range. He bellows and scent-marks trees from a gland on his chest to advertise his presence. The time between mating and the birth of a baby Koala is about 35 days.

▶ Koalas may suffer from a disease called chlamydia*.

At home up in the gumtrees

A Koala relies on its thick fur to protect it from the weather. It curls into a ball to keep warm, or spreads its body out to keep cool. Dark fur on its back absorbs heat, while the lighter fur of its underside reflects heat.

A Koala is well-adapted for life in the branches. It has long limbs and paws with rough pads and sharp claws. Each front paw has two "thumbs", which are opposable to the other three "fingers". The hind feet grip the trunk and support the Koala as its front limbs reach for another hold. The second and third toes are fused and used for grooming. The tail is very reduced.

JIRI LOCHMAN

A male Koala crossing from one tree to another at night. His chest-patch contains scent glands

This young Koala is nearly ready for independence. Young males disperse more widely than females

The biggest burrowers

FACTS

▶ An adult Common Wombat may weigh between 22 and 40 kg. Head and body measure 100 cm and the tail is 2.5 cm long.

▶ A wombat can run at 40 km/h for a short distance.

▶ A wombat's teeth have no roots and keep growing throughout the animal's lifetime.

▶ Common Wombats in the Australian Alps spend 19 hours of each winter day in their burrows. In winter, an alpine wombat may have to dig through snow to reach plants to eat.

▶ Thirty days after mating, the female wombat gives birth to a bean-sized baby weighing one gram.

▶ The baby wombat uses its strong front legs to drag itself into the backward-facing pouch. It attaches to a nipple and stays in the pouch for between six and ten months, then follows its mother for another five to ten months.

People who have spent time with wombats describe them as playful and quick to learn. Their well-developed brains are in contrast to the poorly developed brain of their closest relative, the Koala. Since wombats are mainly active at night and avoid humans, their intelligence is not generally appreciated.

The wombat is one of the largest burrowing animals in the world. An individual may spend two-thirds of its life underground, emerging to eat grasses and other vegetation. Wombats are protected in all States, except in eastern Victoria. The Common Wombat lives in the forests and woodlands of southeastern Australia. The now-rare Northern and Southern Hairy-nosed Wombats lived on open country, where after European settlement cattle, sheep and rabbits competed for grass. The wombats disappeared from most of their ranges and today fewer than 100 Northern Hairy-nosed Wombats remain, located in Epping Forest National Park in central Queensland. Isolated colonies of the Southern Hairy-nosed Wombat live on the Nullarbor Plain and in southern and eastern South Australia.

A wombat has sturdy legs and can walk long distances when foraging

The Northern Hairy-nosed Wombat has silky fur, a hairy muzzle, and longer ears than the Common Wombat

The Common Wombat has a rounded head and strong claws

More than just a home

The burrow protects the wombat from heat, cold, rain and bushfires. It has sleeping chambers lined with leaves and twigs, and there may be a "vestibule", where the

A brown-furred Common Wombat grazing sand-dune plants

wombat waits for dark, just inside an entrance. A wombat can dig about two metres of burrow each night, loosening soil with alternate scoops of its forepaws, then shoving it backwards with its hindlegs. It lies on its side to scratch out the walls and roof. A burrow may be 30 metres long, about 50 centimetres high and 50 centimetres wide and may connect with other burrows to form a network with several entrances. Such a warren may be the work of several generations.

The Common Wombat has a naked muzzle

FACTS

▶ A predator following a wombat into a burrow may find itself crushed against walls or roof by the wombat's rump.

▶ A number of wombats may use a burrow at the same time, but they lead solitary lives except when breeding.

▶ When wombats rest in their burrows, their metabolism* slows to two-thirds of its normal rate.

▶ A Common Wombat may breed at two. It may only live for five years in the wild. Greatest known age for a Common Wombat is 26 years 22 days, for one which died in London Zoo in 1906.

▶ Many gardeners and farmers use electric fences to keep wombats out. "Wombat gates" allow them to pass through fences.

▶ Wombat fur may range from cream to grey, brown, or black.

Northern Hairy-nosed Wombat

Living the high life

FACTS
ABOUT
BRUSHTAIL POSSUMS

▶ The Common Brushtail Possum has a foxy face and its scientific name, *Trichosurus vulpecula*, means "little-fox-like hairy-tail".

▶ A female brushtail has a forward-facing pouch containing two nipples and may breed after she reaches 12 months of age. The autumn and spring breeding seasons are marked by noisy courtships.

▶ A single baby is born 18 days after mating. It spends between four and five months in the pouch, then another one to two months riding on its mother's back before it is weaned.

▶ Male Common Brushtails scent-mark their territory using glands under the chin, on the chest and near the anus. They do not welcome young males trying to establish their own home ranges.

▶ The Common Brushtail was released in New Zealand about 150 years ago and has become a pest in forests there. Its skin supplies a profitable fur trade.

Brushtail Possums, cuscuses and the Scaly-tailed Possum all climb trees and eat vegetation and there are similarities between their skulls and teeth. However, they are different in many other ways.

Brushtail possums have foxy, pointed faces and furry tails. They are agile climbers, though their tails cannot support the weight of their bodies. The "thumb" and the clawless "big toe" can be opposed to the other digits on paw and foot. They are adaptable marsupials, able to survive in different habitats.

A female Common Brushtail Possum and young one

Cuscuses are slow-moving tree-dwellers with flat faces, short ears and naked, scaly, prehensile* tails. Like the Koala, a cuscus has two "thumbs" and its "big toe" can be opposed to the other toes, giving it a secure grip on branches. In Australia, cuscuses are found only in the canopies of Cape York rainforests.

A Mountain Brushtail Possum uses one front paw to hold its food

The elusive Scaly-tailed Possum

Europeans only discovered the existence of the Scaly-tailed Possum in 1917. It was not until 1942 that a second possum was collected for scientific study, then a third in 1954. All came from the Kimberley of Western Australia.

The Scaly-tailed Possum has a tail covered with rasp-like scales, and digits like those of a cuscus, but in many other ways it resembles a brushtail possum. It is found only in isolated places in the Kimberley, where it hides in rocks during the day. At night, it feeds on blossoms, fruits, leaves and insects.

The Worora Aboriginal people of the west coast of the Kimberley accounted for the bare tail of the Scaly-tailed Possum, Ilangurra, by the following story:

"Long ago, Ilangurra had a bushy tail like the ordinary possum. One day, Ilangurra was beginning to climb a tree when a passing Echidna, Koonunginya, seized him by the tail. In trying to pull the possum down, the Echidna pulled all the hair out of his tail. Ilangurra jumped down from the tree and seized Koonunginya and threw him into a prickly bush. Since that day, Ilangurra has had a bare and scaly tail and Koonunginya has been covered with spines."

A Spotted Cuscus, showing its two "thumbs"

The rare Scaly-tailed Possum lives in rocky areas of Western Australia's Kimberley Division

FACTS
ABOUT CUSCUSES

▶ The Spotted Cuscus is found in forests on the tip of Cape York and is widespread in New Guinea.

▶ The Grey Cuscus was only included on the list of Australia's mammals in 1938. It lives in rainforests on the eastern side of Cape York Peninsula and in New Guinea.

▶ Both species of cuscus eat leaves, flowers and fruit. They have large canine teeth and eat some animal food.

▶ Female cuscuses have four nipples in the forward-facing pouch. One or two young ones are reared.

▶ Cuscuses climb slowly and do not leap. Grounded, they move only as fast as a walking human.

▶ Nocturnal tree-living mammals like cuscuses have large eyes set in front of their heads. This gives them binocular vision. Each eye sends the brain a slightly different picture, allowing the animal to judge distances accurately.

DID YOU KNOW?

FACTS
ABOUT
PYGMY-POSSUMS

▶ Most pygmy-possums eat insects, but the Mountain Pygmy-possum stores seeds for winter use and the Eastern Pygmy-possum eats nectar and pollen.

▶ Because of their small size, pygmy-possums find it difficult to maintain body temperature in cold weather. They may become torpid for up to two weeks in winter, or when food is scarce.

▶ Male and non-breeding female Long-tailed Pygmy-possums will share a nest made from leaves. A female may share with her offspring.

▶ The Little Pygmy-possum is the smallest of all the possums, weighing up to 9 g. Head and body may measure 6.5 cm, and the tail 7.5 cm.

▶ The Feathertail Glider (see page 42) is a pygmy-possum which has developed a web of skin between body and legs, allowing it to glide, steered by its long, feathery tail.

The Long-tailed Pygmy-possum is found only in tropical rainforest in North Queensland

Hanging out

Pygmy-possums are mouse-sized climbers which have long, prehensile tails, which they use as fifth limbs. They have a blade-like, projecting upper premolar on each side of the jaw which is used for chomping through hard seeds or tough insects.

Ringtail possums are cat-sized and also have prehensile tails. They have two "thumbs" on each forepaw and climb and leap with agility amongst the treetops where they browse on leaves, fruit and flowers. The Common Ringtail of eastern and southwestern Australia sleeps by day in a leafy nest in a hollow or in a drey* built in the branches. The Green, Herbert River, Daintree and Lemuroid Ringtails are rainforest possums found only in restricted localities in North Queensland. Felling or degradation of rainforest threatens these unique species. The Rock Ringtail of arid northern Australia is unusual in having a short tail. It lives amongst rocks rather than in trees and would gain few benefits from a long, "handy" tail.

Eastern Pygmy-possum feeding on banksia nectar. Small marsupials pollinate many native plants

Burramys, the survivor

The fossilised skull fragments of a tiny marsupial were found in 1895 at Wombeyan Caves, New South Wales. The animal was named *Burramys*, meaning "stony-place-mouse".

In 1966, a "small, friendly possum" turned up in a ski hut on Mount Hotham, Victoria. It was a living *Burramys*, or Mountain Pygmy-possum, the only Australian mammal restricted to alpine and subalpine regions. It even lives on the summit of Mount Kosciusko, at an altitude of 2230 metres.

The Mountain Pygmy-possum eats vegetation and insects. During winter, it scampers around in runways close to the ground. To survive the cold and lack of food, it metabolises* body fat, eats stored seeds and may become torpid. Nesting material is carried in the female's prehensile tail. Four young are born. When only a few weeks old, they leave the pouch and are left in the nest. They reach adult size at five months and breed in their second year.

Burramys, the Mountain Pygmy-possum

A Green Ringtail huddled in sleep (or alarm) posture

Three sociable Rock Ringtails, the youngest on its mother's back

FACTS
ABOUT RINGTAILS

▶ The "green" of the Green Ringtail's fur is actually a combination of black, white and yellow.

▶ The Green Ringtail sleeps curled into a ball, gripping a branch with its feet and sitting on its tightly coiled tail. It curls up like this when alarmed, relying on camouflage* to protect it.

▶ The Rock Ringtail has a shorter tail, shorter legs and shorter claws than tree-living ringtail species.

▶ A Common Ringtail may have up to five spherical nests in its home range.

▶ There are two colour varieties of the Herbert River Ringtail Possum. The southern form has dark, almost black and white fur, the northern form is pale fawn, with a dark stripe on the head.

Coppery Ringtail

Aerial artistes and some solo acts

Amongst mammals, only bats have developed powered flight. Gliders do not fly, but volplane*, or glide, from tree to tree. The largest gliding marsupial, the Greater Glider, is related to the ringtail possums. It can weigh as much as 1.7 kilograms and glides on flaps of skin stretching between elbow and ankle on each side of its fluffy body.

The largest of the group of smaller gliders, all of which which have this patagium* stretching between wrists and ankles, is the Yellow-bellied Glider, which weighs about 500 grams. This glider chews V-shaped or zig-zag notches into bark, then licks up the sap which oozes into the notches. The Squirrel Glider, which weighs up to 250 grams, lives in woodlands in drier areas. Its lookalike, the Sugar Glider, weighing less than 150 grams, is common in forests over eastern and northern Australia. The tiny Feathertail Glider, a pygmy-possum, weighs less than 15 grams.

The rare Leadbeater's Possum resembles a Sugar Glider without gliding membranes.

The Striped Possum is boldly marked in black and white and has a strong odour. It is found in north Queensland rainforests, where it moves at great speed amongst the branches and leaps boldly between trees. It eats some leaves and fruit, but most of its diet is wood-boring insect larvae, which are retrieved with sharp incisors, long tongue and elongated fourth finger.

This Yellow-bellied Glider is licking tree sap

Leadbeater's Possum also eats tree sap

40

The sociable Sugar Glider

The Sugar Glider's scientific name, *Petaurus breviceps*, means "short-headed rope-dancer". A Sugar Glider can glide for at least 50 metres, steering and maintaining stability by varying the curve on the right or left membrane. About three metres from the target tree, it brings its hindlegs to its body and swoops upwards, to land on all four feet. These small gliders feed on nectar, pollen, insects and wattle gum. They live in groups, whose members sleep together in tree-hollows lined with leaves. Group members recognise each other by scent and spend a lot of time exchanging secretions from scent glands. If the male in a group dies, he is usually replaced by a lone male from a nearby territory.

The Mahogany Glider was rediscovered recently

QUEENSLAND MUSEUM

The Sugar Glider eats nectar and insects

Forests for gliders

An "old" forest has plenty of mature trees. The Greater Glider, which eats almost nothing but eucalypt leaves and needs large hollows as refuges, is abundant in such forests.

The endangered Mahogany Glider lives in eucalypts with an understory of wattles. In 1995, the Queensland Government halted clearing of an area of forest in coastal North Queensland which is suitable habitat for this rare glider.

The Greater Glider eats eucalypt leaves

FACTS
THE STRIPED POSSUM

▶ The Striped Possum sleeps during the day in a nest made of leaves placed inside a hollow or clump of ferns.

▶ This boldly marked possum has a strong, sweet, musky odour. It gouges bark away with its lower incisors before extracting a grub with its tongue or sharp claws.

Feathertail Gliders

Furred pollen-couriers

Many of Australia's plants bear nectar-producing flowers which attract mammals.

Banksias, eucalypts, hakeas, dryandras, bottlebrushes and other shrubs and trees provide nectar and nectar-seeking insects for hungry possums, pygmy-possums, rodents and the Honey-possum. Flying-foxes and blossom-bats join gliders and possums to feast at the flowers of bush and rainforest trees.

The animals obtain nectar, protein-rich pollen and a bonus of insects. The flowers have all sorts of mechanisms which deposit pollen on their dinner-guests. This pollen is carried to other flowers and fertilises them.

The long fourth finger on a Striped Possum's paw is used to extract wood-boring insect larvae

THE UNIQUE HONEY-POSSUM

The tiny Honey-possum has the fewest teeth of any marsupial, only a pair of pointed lower incisors and some peg-like simple teeth. It uses its long, brush-tipped tongue to probe flowers for nectar and pollen. The Honey-possum's scientific name, *Tarsipes rostratus*, means "(long-) snouted tarsier*-foot". Like the tarsier and other primates*, it has "fingernails" and "toenails" rather than claws. It grips branches with pads on the ends of its digits* and with a long, prehensile tail. Honey-possums sleep during the day in old bird-nests, or in the hollow stems of grass-trees and in cold weather may become torpid.

A Honey-possum feeding from a hakea flower. It is the sole member of its family

▶ On land, a macropod cannot move its hindlegs alternately and it cannot easily move backwards.

▶ However, when swimming, a macropod kicks its hindlegs alternately.

▶ When moving at speed, a macropod uses its tail to counterbalance its body as its hindlegs swing backwards and forwards.

▶ At speeds above 17 km/h, hopping is more efficient in terms of oxygen consumption than running or galloping.

▶ A large macropod uses its tail as a fifth leg.

MUSKY RAT-KANGAROO, HARE-WALLABIES, POTOROOS AND BETTONGS

Little hoppers with long feet

Macropods* means "great-footed animals". It is the name given to the kangaroos and their relatives, which have powerful hindlegs and long feet. The second and third toes of a macropod's hindfoot are joined together, like those of a bandicoot. All macropods except the Musky Rat-kangaroo hop on their hindlegs when going at speed.

All female macropods have pouches and each has four nipples. Female macropods give birth to one young one or joey at a time (the Musky Rat-kangaroo has twins).

The endangered Long-footed Potoroo

THE 59 SPECIES OF MACROPODS ARE DIVIDED INTO TWO GROUPS.

RAT-KANGAROOS, POTOROOS AND BETTONGS
Small macropods, rarely weighing more than 2 kg, which eat tubers, fungi and bulbs, insects and other small creatures, digging them up with their forelimbs. Most species require dense ground cover and disappear when it is cleared.

KANGAROOS, WALLAROOS, WALLABIES, HARE-WALLABIES, ROCK-WALLABIES, NAILTAIL WALLABIES, PADEMELONS AND QUOKKA
Larger macropods which range in size from the Quokka (3-4 kg) to the Red Kangaroo (up to 85 kg). Grazers and browsers, found in a wide variety of habitats.

The Musky Rat-kangaroo is the smallest macropod

STANLEY BREEDEN

Tiny and unique

The Musky Rat-kangaroo of northern Queensland rainforest is the smallest of all the macropods (males average 500 grams in weight, females less). Unlike other macropods, it has a first toe on its hindfoot, hops rather than bounds, and has twins rather than one joey. It eats fruit and insects, for its stomach is simple compared to the more complex stomachs of other macropods, and cannot digest the tough cellulose* present in many plants.

Rediscovered!

Gilbert's Potoroo was not recorded for 115 years

Gilbert's Potoroo was discovered near Albany, Western Australia, in 1840. A few were collected for scientific study, but after 1879 nothing more was heard of this smallest of the potoroos. In December, 1994, Liz Sinclair of the University of WA and her assistant Adrian Wayne were trapping Quokkas at Two Peoples Bay, near Albany, and caught a Gilbert's Potoroo. No birdwatcher looking for the endangered Noisy Scrub-bird had spotted the nocturnal potoroos. Some later captures were released wearing radio-collars; three animals were kept for study.

The Brush-tailed Bettong prefers dense undergrowth

Vanishing hare-wallabies

In an early European sighting of a marsupial, the English buccaneer William Dampier recorded that he saw the Banded Hare-wallaby on Dirk Hartog Island, off Shark Bay, WA, on 6 August 1699. It now survives only on Bernier and Dorre Islands in Shark Bay. Of the five known species of hare-wallaby, two have become extinct since European settlement, two are very rare and only the Spectacled Hare-wallaby of northern Australia is reasonably common today.

Banded Hare-wallaby

The rare Rufous Hare-wallaby

FACTS

▶ The endangered Long-footed Potoroo was unknown to science until 1980 and may exist only in a small area in eastern Vic.

▶ The Broad-faced Potoroo of southwest WA's wheatbelt was discovered in 1839 and last seen in 1875. It is probably extinct.

▶ Hare-wallabies can survive for some time without drinking. During the day, they shelter in dense vegetation or in short burrows.

▶ The Musky Rat-kangaroo gathers nest material in its mouth, then transfers it to the forepaws. It places the material on the ground in front of the hindfeet, then kicks it back to be gathered and carried in the tail.

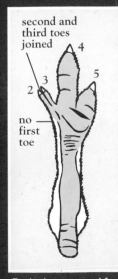

Typical macropod foot

45

Medium-sized macropods

Red-legged Pademelon resting

Red-necked Pademelon with large pouch young

The Warabi is the smallest of the rock-wallabies

The Nabarlek lives in sandstone country

JIRI LOCHMAN

IAN MORRIS

Pademelons

Pademelons are medium-sized macropods with rather short hindfeet, compact bodies and thickish, shortish tails. They live in forests and eat leaves and grass, moving from their resting areas in the forest to their grassy feeding areas and back along runways.

The Red-necked and Red-legged Pademelons are found in suitable habitat on the east coast of mainland Australia. The Tasmanian Pademelon is now extinct on the mainland (it was much hunted for its fur and flesh) and is found only in Tasmania.

Rock-wallabies

Rock-wallabies are amongst the brightest-coloured macropods. They live on rocky outcrops, and the soles of their feet are granulated* to provide friction against rocks.

The tail is used for balancing and is carried arched over the back when the rock-wallaby hops. Rock-wallabies live in colonies numbering from ten to several hundreds. In the past, they moved freely between outcrops, but today this movement is restricted by fences, clearing and predators.

Quokka

The Quokka is a small macropod with a short tail and short hind feet, whose claws are covered by long, stiff hairs.

46

The Quokka, common on Rottnest Island

Black-footed Rock-wallaby

Grass-eaters supreme

The remote ancestors of the macropods were probably tree-living animals which fed on leaves. As rainforests were replaced by open forests and plains, the teeth and stomachs of kangaroos and many of their relatives became adapted to survive on a new diet of grass.

Teeth: A macropod has two bottom incisor teeth, which move past six upper incisors to shear off vegetation. At the back of the mouth are grinding molars. Between incisors and molars is the toothless space called the diastema, which gives the tongue room to press the grass into a wad which is passed back to the molars to be chewed into small fragments for swallowing. Grass contains a hard chemical compound called silica* and as a macropod's foremost molar wears it drops out and another moves forward in the jaw to take its place. Most macropods have four pairs of molars available and if an animal lives a long time only the final molar on each side will be left (see page 54 for a diagram of this in the Euro). However, the little Nabarlek, which eats grass high in silica, produces replacement molars as long as it lives.

Stomach: A herbivore must break down tough plant fibres before it can use the food energy they contain. The stomach of a macropod contains a large chamber in which are bacterial micro-organisms. These ferment plant fibres so their food content can be used by the body.

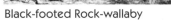

Yellow-footed Rock-wallaby

▶ The Northern Nailtail Wallaby is called the "Organ-grinder Wallaby" because it makes circles with an arm when it hops.

nailtail wallaby tail tip

▶ By the early 1920s, the lovely Toolache was so rare in SE South Australia that concerned people tried to relocate animals on Kangaroo Island. They used dogs to chase the wallabies, which died of stress. The last proven sighting of wild Toolaches was in 1924.

▶ The Red-necked Wallaby is common in coastal woodland from Rockhampton, Queensland, to South Australia.

▶ The Swamp Wallaby browses on coarse-leaved plants, including species such as bracken fern and hemlock which are poisonous to domestic stock.

Wallabies

Wallabies are medium-sized macropods, smaller than kangaroos, which often browse on leaves as well as graze on grass. Wallaby and kangaroo males are often much bigger than females of the same species.

IAN MORRIS

The Northern Nailtail Wallaby has a spur at the end of its tail

Larger wallabies and kangaroos often live in groups and a male's rank may be decided by sparring with other males. The higher a male's status in a mob of wallabies or kangaroos, the more females will mate with him.

Some species of wallaby have grown scarce in the past 200 years. The Toolache, "most beautiful and elegant of all of the wallabies", is extinct and the Crescent Nailtail Wallaby of central Australia has not been reported since the 1950s and is presumed extinct. The Bridled Nailtail is endangered. The Parma Wallaby was thought to be extinct on the Australian mainland by 1932, but had been imported into New Zealand, where it had become a pest. In 1967, the Parma Wallaby was rediscovered in eastern New South Wales. The Northern Nailtail, Red-necked, Pretty-face, Black-striped, Western Brush and Tammar Wallabies seem secure.

Red-necked Wallabies, one with a joey

A special case

The unusual Swamp Wallaby, which is placed by scientists in a macropod group of its own, has teeth adapted to browse on the leafy diet that long-ago macropod ancestors ate. While a female Swamp Wallaby may carry a blastocyst while suckling a baby, the mating which produced this embryo took place up to eight days *before* the current baby's birth, not *after* it, as is usual.

Swamp Wallaby

Tammar made history

Francis Pelsaert, of the *Batavia*, sighted a Tammar on the Abrolhos Islands, off WA, on 15 November 1629. Pelsaert thought the wallaby's young one was born from the nipple. In 1830, London surgeon Alexander Collie watched a Tammar give birth and the tiny baby emerge from the cloaca, crawl unaided to the pouch and enter it. The Tammar can drink sea water if no fresh is available even while suckling a joey.

A male Agile Wallaby resting under a pandanus

FACTS

▶ The Agile Wallaby is the most common wallaby in tropical coastal Australia. It may be declared a pest in some areas, especially around cane farms.

▶ Pretty-face Wallabies live in mobs of up to 50 animals. Within the mob are sub-groups of up to ten adults and young ones.

▶ A Pretty-face Wallaby female gives birth five weeks after mating. The young one detaches from the nipple at about 23 weeks, leaves the pouch at 37 weeks but continues to suckle until about 15 months old.

▶ The Tasmanian form of the Red-necked Wallaby is called Bennett's Wallaby. It has long, dense fur and numbers are killed in open seasons for skins and meat.

Young Pretty-face Wallaby suckling. There may be a second, younger joey attached to another nipple

Bennett's Wallaby

DID YOU KNOW?

FACTS

▶ Tree-kangaroos are the only macropods which can "walk", moving their hindfeet alternately.

▶ On the ground, a tree-kangaroo walks on four legs, or hops on its hind legs.

▶ In a tree, the kangaroo grips a trunk or vertical branch with its strong, clawed forepaws and walks, or runs, forwards or backwards along horizontal branches. The long tail is used as a counterbalance.

▶ A tree-kangaroo will slide down a tree, moving its forelimbs alternately and keeping its feet clamped around the trunk, until about 2 m from the ground. Then it jumps, twists in mid-air to remain upright, lands and bounds off.

▶ A frightened tree-kangaroo may jump to another tree, or drop to the ground from as high as 15 m.

▶ "Monkeys" reported in North Queensland may be tree-kangaroos.

Kangaroos up trees

The remote ancestors of kangaroos probably lived in trees. As Australia grew drier and rainforests retreated, most kangaroos adapted well to living on the ground, while the tree-kangaroos found their preferred leafy diet in the treetops.

Australia's two species of tree-kangaroos, Lumholtz's and Bennett's, live in rainforest on Cape York Peninsula. They have very long, muscular forelimbs and hindfeet which are almost rectangular in shape, with granulated, non-slip soles. Agile climbers, though their tails are not prehensile, they feed on leaves and fruits. Bennett's is the larger species; a male weighs up to 13 kilograms.

Lumholtz's Tree-kangaroo, showing sole of foot

A tree-kangaroo's long tail is not prehensile

Goodfellow's Tree-kangaroo, a New Guinea species

GREY KANGAROOS

The original "kangooroo"

The Eastern and Western Grey Kangaroos are typical of the large grazing macropods.

The Eastern Grey lives in mobs of ten or more down the eastern side of Australia where the annual rainfall is more than 250 millimetres. Its preferred food is grass and it grazes from late afternoon to early morning. Although the species is protected, culling licences may be issued where kangaroos are seen as pests.

The darker-furred Western Grey Kangaroo is found in the south and southwest of Australia. It has shorter periods for pregnancy and pouch-life than the Eastern Grey.

Captain Cook and the kangaroos

Captain James Cook's ship *Endeavour* was beached for repairs at the Endeavour River after sailing onto a coral reef near Cape Tribulation in June 1770. The ship's botanist, Joseph Banks, reported the sighting of "an animal as large as a grey hound, of a mouse colour and very swift" on 22 June 1770. Captain Cook saw his first Grey Kangaroo on 24 June. Two Grey Kangaroos and a Common Wallaroo were shot and Cook wrote that "the Beast which was killd yesterday was today Dressed for our dinners and provd excellent meat." On 4 August, he noted that "...the Animal which I have before mentioned is called by the natives *Kangooroo* or *Kanguru*".

Eastern Grey Kangaroo

FACTS ABOUT GREY KANGAROOS

- A big adult male Eastern Grey Kangaroo may measure over 1 m from its nosetip to the butt of the tail, with a tail up to 1 m long.

- A big female Grey Kangaroo will have a body up to 1 m long and a tail around 80 cm in length.

- A male Eastern Grey Kangaroo may weigh up to 66 kg, a female up to 32 kg.

- The Tasmanian form of the Eastern Grey Kangaroo is known as the Forester Kangaroo.

A mob of Eastern Grey Kangaroos

FACTS
ABOUT GREY KANGAROOS

▶ The highest speed record for a marsupial, 64 km/h, is held by a female Eastern Grey Kangaroo.

▶ There is an unconfirmed record of an Eastern Grey Kangaroo long-jumping 13.5 m.

▶ A captive Eastern Grey Kangaroo cleared a 2.44 m fence when a car backfired.

▶ The scientific name of the Eastern Grey Kangaroo, *Macropus giganteus*, means "giant great-foot".

▶ The scientific name of the darker Western Grey, *Macropus fuliginosus*, means "sooty great-foot".

A pouch young of the Western Grey Kangaroo attached to a nipple

A baby in reserve

A newborn young Eastern Grey Kangaroo weighs under one gram. Born 36 days after mating, it climbs unaided to the pouch and attaches to a nipple, which swells to plug into its mouth. The female will mate again after giving birth, but until the baby leaves the pouch at about 11 months the embryo will not develop inside her. If the suckling baby disappears, the embryo will resume development. A joey is not independent until it is 18 months old, by which time there may be a new pouch young one about eight months old.

JIRI LOCHMAN

A female Eastern Grey Kangaroo with a large pouch young. Note the five "fingers" on her forepaw

Male Eastern Grey Kangaroos test their status in the mob by wrestling and sparring

WALLAROOS

Rocks and hard places

Wallaroos are large, stocky macropods with bare muzzles, which favour rocky hills or an escarpment as habitat. They can survive in arid areas with very little surface water, sheltering during the day in caves or under ledges, grazing at night on nearby plains and slopes. They may dig holes in soaks and dry creekbeds to obtain moisture.

Female Antilopine Wallaroo hopping

STANLEY BREEDEN

In eastern Australia, the Common Wallaroo is dark grey and may be found in forest. In central and western Australia, this species is reddish, lives in hot, arid areas and is known as the "Euro". The Antilopine Wallaroo of northern Australia lives in small groups in open forest and on plains.

The rare Black Wallaroo is found on the rocky Arnhem Land escarpment of the Northern Territory. It is normally solitary and is very wary and difficult to approach.

The wary Black Wallaroo

IAN MORRIS

MOVING MOLARS

As a macropod's front molar wears down, it drops out and is replaced by the molar which lies behind it

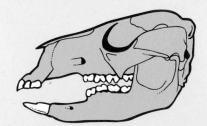

Skull of Euro with all four pairs of molars in wear

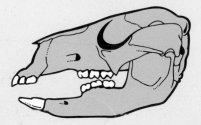

Skull of Euro after the front molars have worn and been shed and the second pair have moved forward

JIRI LOCHMAN

This Euro on Barrow Island, WA, is drinking from a hole dug in the sand

FACTS
ABOUT DESERT SURVIVAL

▶ Macropods do not sweat. If hot, they lick their chests and arms and the evaporating saliva cools blood in surface vessels.

▶ The long roof of a macropod's mouth acts as an evaporative cooler. The cleft upper lip guides moisture from the nose into the mouth. The nostrils can be closed, and the entrances to the ears and eyes are protected by stiff hairs.

▶ Desert macropods shelter during the day and feed at night.

IAN MORRIS

Male Antilopine Wallaroo

A Female Antilopine Wallaroo may weigh 20 kg less than a male Antilopine

▶ Most male Red Kangaroos are pale- to brick-red in colour, while females are usually blue-grey. However, there are blue-grey males, and in some areas females may be reddish.

▶ Almost 50% of young Red Kangaroos fail to reach two years of age; 90% die before the age of ten.

▶ In hot weather, Red Kangaroos "lie up" during the day in the shade at the bases of trees and bushes. They sometimes dig through the surface soil to make a cooler "bed".

Red Kangaroo. When large macropods hop, the tail is used as a counterbalance to the body

RED KANGAROO

The biggest marsupial

The Red Kangaroo is the largest of the macropods. A large male may stand tall as a man and weigh 85 kilograms. It may measure 1.4 metres from the nose to the butt of the tail, while the tail measures one metre. Females are smaller and a young female may weigh less than 20 kilograms.

This kangaroo is found over most of the central part of Australia which receives less than 500 millimetres of rainfall per year. It prefers open plains scattered with trees, under which it rests during the day. It grazes mostly at night and can survive on a minimum of surface water if it can eat some green herbage.

A typical group of Red Kangaroos consists of a dominant male, a number of adult females and some juveniles. Females may breed at between 15 and 20 months of age and males at two years, though both continue to increase in body size for some years afterwards. Females are fertile throughout the year when food is plentiful, but cease to come into breeding condition in drought years.

A large male Red Kangaroo with (right) a grey female and (left) a reddish female

A female Red Kangaroo licks her paws and forearms to cool herself on a hot day

Young Red Kangaroos wrestling

FACTS

▶ A male Red Kangaroo was timed at 56 km/h for 1.6 km. The kangaroo died of stress after its effort.

▶ A hunted female Red Kangaroo made a long-jump of 12.8 m.

▶ A hunted male "Big Red" cleared a stack of timber 3.1 m high.

Male Red Kangaroo

Megabats

FACTS

- Flying-foxes were so-called because their heads were thought to resemble those of foxes.

- Flying-foxes have good nocturnal vision and find food by sight, by scent, and by following the loud feeding-cries of other bats.

- Each species of flying-fox has its own strong odour.

- Flying-foxes may skim over water to drink.

- The scientific name of the Grey-headed Flying-fox, *Pteropus poliocephalus*, means "grey-headed wing-foot".

- Megabats play a large part in the pollination of trees and the distribution of their seeds.

A Spectacled Flying-fox roosts with its wings wrapped around its body

Bats are placental mammals, whose young remain inside their mothers' bodies until they are well-developed. There are two very different kinds of bats found in Australia, "megabats" and "microbats".

Megabats are larger than microbats and include flying-foxes and blossom-bats. They do not use echolocation to navigate, nor to locate food. A megabat has big eyes and simple ears and its muzzle is quite long and foxy. The tail is short or absent and the leading edge of the wing has two claws.

Megabats roost during the day, often in a "camp". Each bat hangs by its feet with its wings wrapped around its body, holding its head at right angles to its chest.

Most megabats prefer blossoms, but will eat fruit, which is crushed between the jaws. The bat then swallows the juice and spits out most of the pulp. The gut is short and simple and food passes through it very quickly.

Babies with wings

Black Flying-foxes mate in March and April and the young one is born in October. It cannot fly and is carried by its mother for about a month, gripping fur and a nipple with its claws and recurved milk teeth. At about one month, it is left in camp at night while its mother flies off to feed. It can fly at two months of age, but does not venture out of camp for another month.

A mob of Little Red Flying-foxes leaves camp

STANLEY BREEDEN

Black Flying-fox and young

STANLEY BREEDEN

Are megabats primates?

There are many differences between the fruit-eating megabats and the insectivorous microbats. Some scientists believe that the two groups are not closely related at all and did not have a common ancestor. They feel that the similarities between megabats and microbats are simply the result of two groups of mammals becoming adapted to flight in much the same way. The megabats are seen as being related to the primates, the group to which humans, apes, tarsiers and lemurs belong.

Snorkels or scenters?

Tube-nosed bats have large, protruding, elegantly scrolled nostrils. Once they were thought to act as snorkels while the owner ate mushy fruit. Present thinking is that each nostril picks up scent at a slightly different angle, giving the bat a directional "fix" on a food source.

FACTS

▶ Megabats can weigh up to 1 kg or more and may have a wingspan of up to 1.6 m. They have claws on the first and second fingers of the forelimb.

▶ Megabats can live only in tropical and temperate climates, where the fruit and flowers of their diet can be found all year around. They may have to fly great distances to find food.

▶ Blossom-bats feed on pollen and nectar, using tongues which have brush-like projections.

Spectacled Flying-fox preparing for takeoff

Queensland Blossom-bat

STANLEY BREEDEN

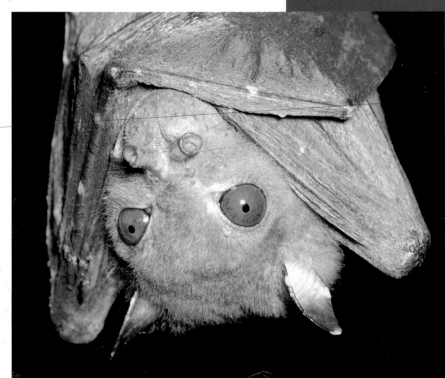

Queensland Tube-nosed Bat

STANLEY BREEDEN

DID YOU KNOW?

FACTS
ABOUT HIBERNATION

A microbat has a large body surface to lose heat and uses a lot of energy in flight. In cold weather, it may become torpid or hibernate. A hibernating bat has a body temperature only a few degrees above that of its surroundings.

When awakening from hibernation, a bat must spend some time "exercising" before it can fly. Bats often hibernate on very limited food reserves. If wakened prematurely, they may use so much energy they cannot survive further hibernation.

Some female microbats mate before hibernating. When a female revives, one of the sperm stored in her body fertilises an egg-cell. In other species, the egg-cell is fertilised after mating, but does not develop further until the female revives from hibernation.

A microbat receiving back sound reflected from a moth

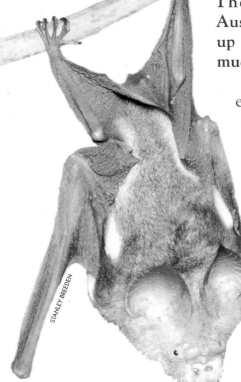

The Diadem Horseshoe-bat has a regular hunting track, where it waits in ambush, scanning for possible prey with ultrasound

STANLEY BREEDEN

Microbats

The largest of the world's microbats, Australia's Ghost Bat, may have a wingspan of up to 60 centimetres, but most microbats are much smaller.

Microbats have small eyes and many have elaborate external ears and noseleaves, associated with their use of echolocation* to hunt and to navigate. The forelimb of a microbat has only one claw. When the bat is hanging upside down, its wings are usually folded against the sides of its body. Its head hangs downwards, or is raised to make a right angle with its back. Except for the Ghost Bat, which eats small vertebrates*, including other bats, all the Australian microbats are insectivorous. The Large-footed Myotis is a "fishing bat", which rakes up insects from the surface of swamps and lakes with its feet.

Echolocation

Many bats send out up to 200 pulses of high-pitched ultrasound* per second, produced by the larynx* and projected through the mouth or nostrils. Pulses received back are collected by the large external ears, then the bat's brain makes a "picture" of the objects which reflected the pulses. A flap across the ear of some species, the tragus*, helps the bat pinpoint directions. Bats emit different pulses according to whether they are cruising, locating prey or chasing it.

IAN MORRIS

The Large-footed Myotis's tail is enclosed in membrane

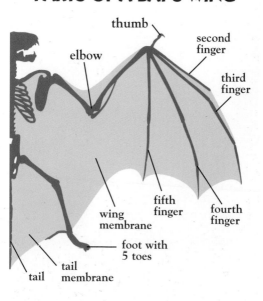

PARTS OF A BAT'S WING

thumb

second finger

elbow

third finger

fifth finger

fourth finger

wing membrane

foot with 5 toes

tail

tail membrane

Ghost Bat

STANLEY BREEDEN

Long-eared bats have large ears which aid echolocation. The wide-opening jaws engulf flying insects

Australia's Ghost Bat

The rare Ghost Bat, the largest microbat in the world, is found only in Australia. It has large eyes, large ears with a tragus, and an elaborate noseleaf. It uses echolocation, though it does not emit signals constantly. A bat hangs in wait, then flies out to catch a night-flying bird, bat or ground animal, enveloping the animal in its wings, biting to kill it, then carrying it to a feeding site. Ghost Bats roost in small groups in caves and old mine shafts. Females form separate nursery colonies and bring food back to their young ones.

STANLEY BREEDEN

A nursery of Little Bent-wing Bat babies in a storm drain

Good-looking rats

Rodents* make up half of the world's approximate total of 4000 mammal species. Larger rodents are generally called "rats", while smaller ones are called "mice".

Compact-bodied animals with razor-sharp incisor teeth, rodents have keen senses. They are intelligent and adaptable, with front paws which may be used for grasping food and other objects. Their efficient digestive systems are capable of utilising 80 per cent of the energy content of food eaten.

The Grassland Melomys builds its nest in native grasses

The first rodents reached Australia between 10 and 15 million years ago. A second "wave" came to the continent no later than one million years ago. By 1788, nearly one-quarter of Australia's mammal species were rodents, including some which, like the hopping-mice, were adapted to very dry habitats. European humans transported to the continent the House Mouse and two species of rat. All three rodents flourished. Today, some sort of rodent is to be found in every Australian environment.

Rodents gnaw for their lives

The word "rodent" means "gnawer". A rodent has one large pair of incisor teeth in the upper jaw and one pair in the lower. The front surface of each incisor tooth is protected by tough, wear-resisting enamel, which forms a chisel-edge as the softer dentine which covers the rest of the tooth wears away.

The incisors continue to grow throughout a rodent's lifetime, and are ground away on gnawed material and against each other. If an incisor is misaligned, its opposite number will continue to grow unopposed and may circle and eventually pierce the owner's skull. Behind the incisors on each side of the rodent jaw is an open space, the diastema. The lips can be drawn into this to form a barrier between the rodent's throat and gnawed debris.

Fawn-footed Melomys shows its incisors   IAN MORRIS

62

Water-rat feeding on a dead fish

The Bush Rat lives in coastal southern Australia

The Brush-tailed Rabbit-rat lives in trees

Nature's food-chain

The Long-haired Rat of Central Australia breeds to "plague" numbers after sustained good rains in the desert. Rats spread out over the country, seeking food and shelter (Burke and Wills noted such an explosion of numbers in 1860).

Predators such as birds of prey, foxes, cats and snakes congregate and feed on the Long-haired Rats and other small mammals.

Letter-winged Kites, rare white hawks which hunt at night like owls, gather to feed on the rats. They may bring up several broods of chicks before rat numbers "crash" as the country dries and food supplies decrease. The kites feed their final brood on lizards, though hungry feral cats may eat the kite chicks and take over the empty nests. Many kites starve, but a nucleus of rats and predators remains throughout the dry years that follow, ready to breed up when substantial rains fall again on the arid country.

The night-hunting Letter-winged Kite's life story is tied to the boom-and-bust cycles of the Long-haired Rat

All sorts of mice

Since Europeans settled in Australia, seven species of native rodents (four hopping-mice, one mouse, one tree-rat and one stick-nest rat) have become extinct.

Around 12 other species of native rodents are endangered. Some have suffered from habitat destruction or disturbance, others from competition from introduced rats and the House Mouse, or from predation by cats and foxes. When the family cat brings in a mouse or rat, even in city suburbs, close examination may reveal that it is a native species.

Spinifex Hopping-mouse takes refuge in burrows

Twice-digested food

A rodent is able to digest the cellulose in plant fibre by eating one meal twice. Below the stomach is a large caecum, which houses micro-organisms. These split the fibre into digestible carbohydrates (starches and sugars), which can only be absorbed into the body in the stomach. A rodent will eat the faecal pellets which contain carbohydrates, so the material passes through its stomach again.

The Ash-grey Mouse of southwestern WA is slightly larger than a House Mouse

FACTS

- The "plagues" of mice which occur in farming country consist of the introduced House Mouse and not of native rodents.

- A number of Australian mice in the group *pseudomys*, which means "false-mouse", resemble the House Mouse. Most species are adapted to desert living.

- One *pseudomys*, Gould's Mouse, is extinct and a number of other species are vulnerable to habitat change or classified as rare and endangered.

- The New Holland Mouse of coastal New South Wales and southern Victoria was "lost" for over 100 years until it was rediscovered in Ku-ring-gai Chase National Park, near Sydney, in 1967.

- The Ash-grey Mouse lives in sandy coastal areas of southwest WA. It must survive for between four and seven months each year without access to free water, and adds moisture-containing insects to its diet during this time.

Calaby's Pebble-mound Mouse

IAN MORRIS

Western Pebble-mound Mouse

JIRI LOCHMAN

Stone homes

In the Pilbara of WA, piles of small rounded stones mark past or present homes of the rare Western Pebble-mound Mouse. A mound may cover from half a square metre to nine square metres and contains U-shaped tunnels. Several generations of mice build a mound, carrying pebbles in their mouths and shuffling them into position with their forelimbs. An adult mouse, smaller than a House Mouse, weighs approximately 10 grams, and the average weight of the pebbles used in constructing the mound is about 5 grams. The Central Pebble-mound Mouse of Central Australia was first recorded in 1985. Other new discoveries are Calaby's Pebble-mound Mouse of Kakadu and another species from inland Queensland.

Hopping-mice

Hopping-mice occur in arid country, where they live in deep burrows and emerge at night to eat seeds, plant shoots and insects. Most species obtain their water needs from their food, and water is conserved in several ways. Spinifex Hopping-mice huddle together during the day, creating a humid microclimate in the nest; the female may recycle water by drinking the urine produced by her suckling young. If no fresh water is available, the Fawn Hopping-mouse can drink salt water, excreting excess salt in its urine. Unfortunately, four of the nine known species of hopping-mice are extinct and two more species are considered to be endangered.

FACTS

▶ The smallest *pseudomys* is the Delicate Mouse of northern Australia, which is about half the weight of a House Mouse. Its head and body measure between 5 and 8 cm and its tail is the same length.

▶ Another *pseudomys*, the Long-tailed Mouse of Tasmania's wet, cold Antarctic beech rainforests, has a tail one and one-half times the length of its body. Male and female mate for life and with their offspring make a home under fallen timber.

A Spinifex Hopping-mouse in action

M. & I MORCOMBE

Sea-swimmers with flipper-feet

Australian Sea-lion scratching with a hind flipper

Seals and sea-lions belong to a group called pinnipeds*, which means "wing-footed animals". They spend much of their time in the water and all four limbs are modified into broad flippers. The arm and leg bones are short and contained inside the body; the hands and feet have become flippers.

A pinniped's body is streamlined and flexible, with projections reduced to a minimum. The head is rounded, the external ears tiny or non-existent and there is little constriction at the neck. The outline is smoothed by a layer of fat or blubber that lies just below the skin. The female's milk glands form a sheet that spreads smoothly over the belly and flanks and the nipples can be retracted to lie flush with the body.

The thick fur and sleek guard-hairs of pinnipeds insulate their bodies

HOW SEALS MOVE

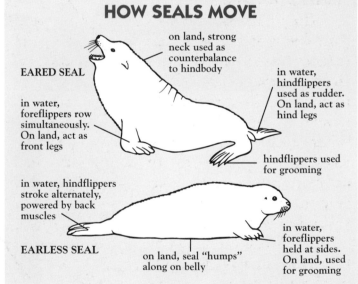

EARED SEAL

on land, strong neck used as counterbalance to hindbody

in water, foreflippers row simultaneously. On land, act as front legs

in water, hindflippers used as rudder. On land, act as hind legs

hindflippers used for grooming

in water, hindflippers stroke alternately, powered by back muscles

EARLESS SEAL

on land, seal "humps" along on belly

in water, foreflippers held at sides. On land, used for grooming

Young Australian Sea-lion suckling

Eared seals and earless seals

The eared seals and the Walrus form a group quite distinct from the earless seals. Both groups are thought to have split off from ancestral carnivore stock, the eared seals about 35 million years ago and the earless seals about 15 million years ago. They adapted their land-living bodies to life in the water, but they are still tied to land or to ice to give birth.

Eared seals such as sea-lions and fur-seals "row" through the water with broad foreflippers and use both sets of flippers for support on land.

Earless seals such as elephant seals swim using alternate strokes of their hindflippers. On land they "hump" along on their bellies.

Freeze or fry

Seals swim in sea water which is much colder than blood temperature.

They have large bodies with few projections, which reduces heat loss and under their skin is a thick insulating layer of fatty blubber. Fur-seals' coats are water-repellent and have an insulating undercoat of dense fur. Hair-seals' coats trap an insulating layer of water against the skin.

Eared seals can only lose heat from the naked surfaces of their flippers. To lose heat, "shunts" in the blood vessels are dilated to increase blood flow to the flippers, which are fanned to help heat loss. When it is necessary to minimise heat loss, the blood flow to the flippers is decreased by shutting off the shunts in the blood vessels.

Australian Fur-seals hunting underwater

A colony of Australian Fur-seals

Female Southern Elephant Seal. This is an earless seal

▶ Dolphins cooperate in hunting, encircling shoals of fish or driving them to shallows.

▶ A pod of about one dozen dolphins may be part of a larger group of several hundred animals.

▶ Dolphins may "spy-hop" up from the water, looking around, before heading towards where seabirds are hovering over a school of fish.

DOLPHINS

In a world of sea-sounds

Dolphins, porpoises and whales make up a group called cetaceans* ("whale-like animals"), which spend their whole lives in the sea. A cetacean is streamlined and has no obvious neck or shoulders. The hindlimbs have been lost and the pelvis is reduced. The arm bones are short and flattened and the fingers are enclosed in tissue to form flippers. The animal swims with powerful up-and-down movements of its horizontal tail flukes*. A layer of blubber under the smooth skin acts as insulation and as a food reserve.

Dolphins are small, torpedo-shaped, toothed cetaceans, which catch fish and other prey using between 100 and 200 sharply pointed teeth. At the top of the head is a single nostril or blowhole. In the forehead of most species is a fatty, oil-filled "melon", used in echolocation. In the midline of a dolphin's back is a triangular dorsal fin which serves as a stabiliser. To prevent the ribcage being crushed by water pressure as a dolphin or other cetacean dives, some of the ribs "float" at one end, while others are jointed and collapse under pressure, later springing back into place.

The world's five species of river dolphins live in fresh water, while the remaining 26 species of dolphins are marine. Porpoises are small dolphins which lack an elongated nose or "beak". None of the world's six species of porpoises is found in Australian waters.

Dolphins are sociable creatures which often live in groups called pods. They communicate with each other using high-pitched whistles.

Bottlenosed Dolphins at sea, showing their dorsal fins and the blowhole of the animal on the right

At several places around Australia's coastline, wild Bottlenosed Dolphins gather to interact with humans

The Bottlenosed Dolphin has a slender snout

Meeting dolphins

Dolphins are highly social and intelligent mammals, which seem to enjoy the company of humans. There are many stories of dolphins "helping" distressed human swimmers (if a dolphin is injured, others of its pod will support it and lift it to the surface so it can breathe). At various beaches around Australia, Bottlenosed Dolphins regularly come to shore to interact with humans. At some places they are fed, at others they make contact without food reward.

SKELETON OF BOTTLENOSED DOLPHIN

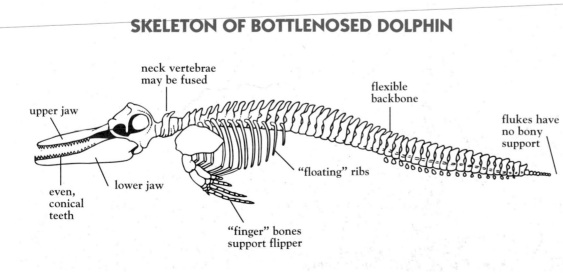

upper jaw

neck vertebrae may be fused

flexible backbone

flukes have no bony support

even, conical teeth

lower jaw

"floating" ribs

"finger" bones support flipper

FACTS

▶ A dolphin breathes through its blowhole, a single, crescent-shaped nostril on the top of its head. Muscles attached to the skull open the blowhole. It closes automatically when the dolphin goes underwater.

▶ A dolphin's eyes function independently of each other. A dolphin can see straight ahead, while a whale has a blind spot directly in front of it.

▶ A dolphin's skin and blubber are attached to each other by small projections. This allows the skin to ripple as the dolphin swims, reducing drag from the water.

▶ Because a dolphin's bones do not have to support its body weight, they are quite soft and porous.

▶ Babies of some dolphin species are born with soft stubble on their body, but this soon disappears.

▶ Some adult cetaceans have bristles on their heads.

DID YOU KNOW?

FACTS

▶ A female Bottlenosed Dolphin in Shark Bay, WA, wore a sea sponge to protect her sensitive snout when she foraged on the seabed. Her calf was observed imitating her, poking its nose into a sponge and swimming around wearing it.

▶ Much of the dolphin's large and complex brain is taken up with "picturing" objects through analysing returning echoes.

▶ Marine dolphins are declining in numbers and urgently need protection.

▶ Every year in the eastern tropical Pacific, at least 100 000 dolphins drown in nets used to round up yellowfin tuna.

▶ For years, the sea has been used as a dumping ground for all sorts of toxic chemical wastes. Mass deaths of dolphins in the North Sea, the Mediterranean and off the east coast of the USA are attributed to this pollution.

▶ All five species of the world's river dolphins are threatened with extinction.

Seeing by sound

Dolphins use their own form of echolocation to find out about their surroundings and to locate fish, squid and other prey.

A dolphin produces clicking noises in the space below its blowhole. (There may be as many as 700 clicks per second, which the human ear would hear as a rusty hinge squeaking.) The clicks pass out as sound waves through the fatty melon on the forehead and fan out like a beam from a torch. The sound waves bounce off a target and are reflected back to the dolphin's lower jaw. From the jaw, they travel to the middle ear, which sends a signal to the brain.

Using echolocation, a Bottlenosed Dolphin can locate a tennis ball-sized object from over 100 metres away.

ECHOLOCATION AS USED BY DOLPHINS

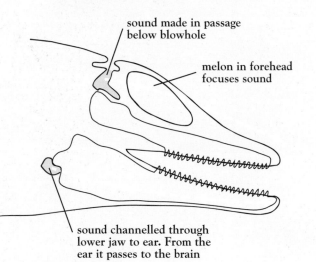

sound made in passage below blowhole

melon in forehead focuses sound

sound channelled through lower jaw to ear. From the ear it passes to the brain

A dolphin is born

Male dolphins are ready to mate between ten and 12 years of age, females between five and 12. Females produce one offspring every two or three years.

Bottlenosed Dolphins mate face-to-face. Pregnancy lasts 12 months and halfway through this period the expectant mother chooses another female as "midwife" and they become a pair.

A baby dolphin is born tail-first. The birth may take two hours, during which time the "midwife" may support the mother. The new baby, which weighs about 25 kilograms and is about one-sixth of the size of its mother, has no air in its lungs and would sink if not held up in the water. Its mother lifts it to the surface to take its first breath.

The mother's two nipples, which are hidden in slits near her tail, are pushed out for the baby to suckle. When the baby wraps its tongue around a nipple, the mother squirts milk into its mouth.

The young one doubles its birth weight in two months and is suckled for up to 18 months, although it begins to eat fish at four months. It learns from its mother and will imitate her in social contacts and food-finding.

When a dolphin raises its forebody from the surface to look around it is said to be "spy-hopping"

JIRI LOCHMAN

Giants of Earth's oceans

There are two groups of cetaceans:

The **toothed whales** feed on fish, squid and other large marine animals. This group includes nearly 90 per cent of all the cetaceans and includes dolphins, porpoises, the sperm whales and the Killer Whale.

The **baleen whales** feed on tiny marine organisms by taking a mouthful of water, raising the tongue and forcing the water through curtains of baleen growing down from each side of the roof of the mouth. Bristles on the inner edges of the baleen strain out the food. Baleen whales include the largest animal on earth, the Blue Whale. Some baleen whales, known as **rorqual whales,** have pleated throats, which expand as water is taken in, then contract again to force the water over the baleen. The Humpback Whale is a rorqual whale which breeds in winter in Australia's subtropical and tropical waters after migrating from its feeding grounds in the Antarctic Ocean.

Species of whale sighted in Australian waters include the Humpback Whale, the Southern Right Whale, the Killer Whale, the Pilot Whale, the Sperm Whale, the Minke Whale and the Southern Blue Whale.

SKELETON OF BALEEN WHALE

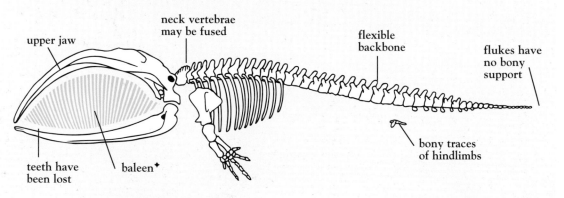

upper jaw

neck vertebrae may be fused

flexible backbone

flukes have no bony support

teeth have been lost

baleen✦

bony traces of hindlimbs

✦ Baleen has developed from the ridges on the roof of the mouth. It is not bone but very tough skin.

The singing Humpback Whale

The Humpback Whale's scientific name, *Megaptera*, means "great-winged". A 15-metre whale may have flippers each five metres in length. A large female Humpback may weigh 65 tonnes and a male slightly less. When a male Humpback reaches the breeding areas off the east and west coasts of Australia, it sings a song which lasts from six to 35 minutes and may be heard underwater up to 185 kilometres away. All males in an area sing the same song, though individual versions are recognisable. The song changes from season to season. Males gather around females to compete for their attention and may leap from the water and roll in mid-air. After mating, the whales migrate to the Antarctic and spend three to four months feeding on krill (small shrimp-like animals), then swim north again. A female gives birth just under 12 months after mating. The young one suckles for seven months and stays with its mother for up to three years.

DID YOU KNOW?

FACTS

▶ Sperm whales are toothed whales which feed on deepwater squid. A Sperm Whale tooth may be 20 cm long and weigh 1 kg. A wax-filled organ in a Sperm Whale's head may direct sound for echolocation.

▶ *Moby Dick*, a classic novel by Herman Melville, tells of the pursuit of a great white Sperm Whale by the relentless Captain Ahab.

▶ The Blue Whale, a rorqual whale, is one of the largest animals ever to have lived on earth, more than 35 m long and weighing around 190 tonnes. It eats 4 million krill every day.

▶ The Southern Right Whale is a baleen whale which may head-stand, waving its flukes, for up to two minutes.

▶ 114 Pilot Whales stranded on a WA beach in 1986.

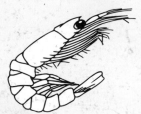

Krill are 7.5 cm long

Tail-thrashing is used by males to intimidate rivals

The delicately fretted edge of a Humpback Whale's tail

Male Humpback Whale shows its enormous flipper and pleated throat as it rises from the sea

Gentle seagrass grazer

FACTS

▶ A large Dugong may be over 3 m in length and weigh 450 kg.

▶ A Dugong's skin has scattered, short sensory bristles.

DUGONG SKULL

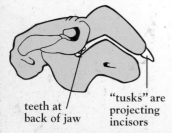

teeth at back of jaw

"tusks" are projecting incisors

The Dugong, the only remaining herbivorous mammal which lives entirely in the sea, is found in shallow, warm coastal waters from Shark Bay, Western Australia, to Moreton Bay, Queensland. It is related to the three living species of freshwater manatees, but its nearest relative was Stellar's Sea Cow, which was discovered by Europeans in the northern Pacific Ocean in 1741. This enormous animal, which weighed up to six times as much as its modern relatives, was hunted vigorously and became extinct by 1768.

A dense skeleton keeps a Dugong on the seabed as it grazes, digging up the carbohydrate-rich roots of smaller seagrass species. Its broad, trunk-like snout ends in a mobile disc covered with bristles, which are used to rake food back into the mouth, where it is chewed by rough horny pads on upper and lower palates. An adult has only a few peg-like molar teeth, though the male has a pair of tusk-like upper incisors, which are possibly used in courtship and to hold the female while mating takes place.

The Dugong's powerful tail, with its horizontal flukes, can propel the animal at up to 22 kilometres per hour. Its paddle-like forelimbs are used for steering, feeding and pushing the animal along the seabed.

A female Dugong with a young one riding on her back. A suckerfish is clinging to the female's belly

GEOFF TAYLOR

The vanishing Dugong

The Dugong is vulnerable to destruction of the seagrass on which it feeds, to being caught in nets, and to hunting. Where it has not been harassed and food is plentiful, the Dugong may live in large herds. Individuals are alert and may treat humans with friendly curiosity.

The world's three manatee species are regarded as endangered and the Dugong is declining in numbers.

A Dugong with suckerfish on its side and belly, and other accompanying fish

A baby Dugong rides above its mother's back

FACTS

▶ Dugongs do not use echolocation.

▶ Average time of a Dugong dive is 76 secs, but one individual remained submerged for nearly 8.5 mins.

▶ Dugong pregnancy lasts about 12 months. A small young one rides on its mother's back except when suckling. It may stay with its mother for up to two years.

▶ Dugongs have only foreflippers, which have no nails. The hindlimbs have been lost, and there are only traces of the pelvic girdle.

▶ Dugongs and manatees belong to a group called "sirenians". The name refers to a fancied resemblance to mermaids, which were also known as sirens.

▶ Old male Dugongs make whistling sounds which may keep the herd together.

▶ A Dugong may live for more than 55 years.

Australia's wild dog

Unlike domestic dogs, the female Dingo has only one breeding cycle per year and a Dingo's teeth and skull differ from those of domestic dogs. Its most likely ancestor is the Indian Plains Wolf.

No Dingo fossil found in Australia so far has been reliably dated to more than 3500 years before the present. Possibly the Dingo was introduced to Australia by seafarers from Southeast Asia. Dingos live in a well-defined home range, which may be shared with others or overlap other ranges. Individuals hunt small game on their own, but join to take larger prey. A group may consist of a breeding pair and younger animals. Dingos interbreed with domestic dogs.

The Dingo and the Aboriginal people

The Dingo appears in Aboriginal art, in some places replacing older depictions of the Thylacine. Aboriginal legends frequently feature the Dingo and the Kundi-Dju-mindju men of the Top End of the Northern Territory dance the story of how the Dingo came ashore from a vessel in the Dreamtime. In other Aboriginal groups, the wild, uncontrollable aspects of the Dingo are celebrated in stories which point out the necessity for order in Aboriginal society. However, the Walbiri people of the Tanami Desert believed that the camp Dingos gave warning of the presence of the Djanbar, malevolent night-time spirits.

A Dingo pack may consist of a dominant male and female and four or five offspring of previous matings

A mature male Dingo weighs about 15 kilograms, approximately the same as a trim Kelpie dog

FACTS

▶ A fence intended to stop rabbits spreading westwards failed to fulfil its purpose. It was continued to prevent easy movement of Dingos as sheep spread.

▶ Today, the Dingo Fence stretches nearly 6000 km from Queensland's Darling Downs to the Great Australian Bight.

▶ In areas where the Dingo is seen as a threat to sheep, it is trapped, shot and poisoned. In these areas, feral rabbits, feral pigs, feral goats and kangaroos, all of which destroy pasture, increase.

▶ Yellow-ginger is a dominant colour in Dingos, but black and tan, all-black, and white purebreds occur.

A black and tan Dingo

Helping Australia's mammals survive

Very few of Australia's native mammals, except for a few larger macropods, have prospered in the past 200 years. Some species are extinct, others will become extinct if their very limited habitat is changed. Some efforts are being made to breed captive stocks of animals such as the Greater Bilby, but reintroduction into the wild will fail while their habitat remains degraded and introduced predators are uncontrolled. Every small effort we can make to assist Australia's unique mammals is worth while. We can...

• Learn as much about Australian mammals as possible, from reading and observation. Find out which mammals are in no danger, which are rare and which are in immediate danger of extinction.

• Leave as much natural vegetation as possible when developing land, and preserve dead trees or branches with hollows which form homes for mammals such as gliders. When landscaping, preference should be given to Australian natives.

• Be aware that gliders and many other Australian mammals need "corridors" linking areas of bush, so that young ones can safely reach new territory when they leave their families.

• Encourage zoos, wildlife sanctuaries and wildlife parks to maintain breeding groups of Australian mammals. Support attempts to re-establish excess offspring from these breeding programmes in their natural habitats, if these areas are suitable.

• Drive with care where mammals are likely to be on roads, especially at night. Animals dazzled by headlights may "freeze".

• Examine recently killed marsupials for pouch young, which may be old enough for hand-rearing. Find a carer by contacting the State National Parks and Wildlife Service.

• Take an informed interest in "commercial" and "pest" species of native animals. Find out why and how they are killed and what use is made of the carcasses.

• Realise that a small mammal observed in the bush or in the garden, or killed by a cat, dog or car, may be a marsupial or a native rodent. If a dead small mammal looks unusual, the body should be wrapped in plastic, frozen, then shown to the mammal expert at the local Museum.

• Reduce the possibility of domestic dogs and cats killing mammals by keeping them in at night. This reduces predation on small mammals and birds, especially by cats. Avoid dumping unwanted kittens. Support elimination of feral animals, especially foxes and cats.

• Observe bushfire precautions.

• Lobby State and Federal Governments to extend parks and reserves and to protect native species. Support local, State and Federal conservation bodies.

• Use poison baits, other pesticides or herbicides with care, so their effects are limited. Remember that some poisons kill not only their target but any animal which then eats the victim.

• Stay alert, be aware of their habits and discover native mammals in all sorts of places.

Study of the rare Western Quoll may help it survive in the wild

STANLEY BREEDEN

JIRI LOCHMAN

Glossary

anaerobic. Without using oxygen.

blastocyst. Embryo at early stage of development, before organs are formed, when it consists of a hollow ball of cells.

caecum. Blind pouch in the digestive canals of many mammals. Especially well developed in herbivores.

camouflage. Protective coloration which blends with background.

carnivore. Animal which eats other animals, e.g. Dingo.

cellulose. Material which makes up cell walls of plants.

cetaceans. Group of ocean mammals which includes whales, dolphins and porpoises.

chlamydia. Disease which affects Koalas, one form of which may lead to reproductive tract infection and reduced fertility.

cloaca. Final part of gut in vertebrate animals (e.g. amphibians, reptiles, birds), except for placental mammals.

dasyurids. Group of carnivorous/insectivorous Australian marsupials which includes quolls, phascogales, antechinuses, Tasmanian Devil, dunnarts etc.

diastema. Toothless space between front cutting teeth and rear grinding teeth found in grazing and browsing animals.

digit. Finger or toe.

diprotodont. Having only one functional pair of incisors in the lower jaw. Typical of herbivore dentition.

drey. Spherical nest made of twigs and leaves.

echolocation. Sensing objects by sending out sounds then analysing the echoes reflected after they impact.

ecological niche. The place a living creature occupies in a community of plants and animals.

embryo. Young animal from conception to birth or hatching.

endothermic. "Warm-blooded". Producing body heat by means of chemical reactions. Typical of birds and mammals.

feral. Having gone back to the wild state.

fluke. Either half of the triangular tail of a whale.

gestation period. Period of time from conception to birth.

granulated. Covered with bumps, grains or granules.

habitat. Place where a particular animal or plant lives or grows. Area where a species is able to survive.

herbivore. Animal which eats mainly vegetable matter, e.g. wombat, wallaby.

hibernation. Period of prolonged inactivity and lowered metabolism brought about by cold weather.

incubate. Keep eggs warm so they develop and hatch.

insectivore. Animal which eats mainly insects, e.g. dunnart.

invertebrate. An animal without a backbone.

larynx. Part of windpipe containing vocal cords.

macropods. Group of herbivorous Australian marsupials with strong hindlegs, which includes kangaroos and wallabies.

mammary glands. Milk-producing glands characteristic of mammals.

marsupial. Mammal with no placenta, whose young are born at embryonic stage after short gestation period, then attach to a nipple, usually within a marsupium, or under folds of skin.

marsupium. Pouch of skin on belly enclosing nipples.

metabolises. Sustains life by chemical processes.

metabolism. Chemical processes which sustain life.

micro-organisms. Minute living creatures such as bacteria and protozoa. Their activity in the digestive system breaks down plant cellulose so the body can use the products.

monotreme. Mammal which lays eggs and possesses a cloaca. It feeds its young on milk but lacks nipples.

native. An animal or plant species belonging to the land, as distinguished from foreign species.

omnivore. Animal which eats plants and animals.

oxygen debt. High level of oxygen consumption needed to pay "debt" owed to body after anaerobic exercise.

patagium. Membrane stretching down both sides of body. Varying its area and position allows animal to glide through the air with some control of direction and angle of descent.

pinnipeds. Group of carnivorous mammals adapted to marine life, including seals and sea-lions.

placenta. Structure connecting circulatory system of unborn infant to that of its mother. It prevents the mother's body rejecting the embryo as a "foreign body".

placental mammal. Mammal whose young, through the presence of a placenta, can remain within the mother's body until their development is complete.

polyprotodont. Having more than one pair of lower incisor teeth. Typical of carnivore and insectivore dentition.

predator. Animal which kills and eats another animal.

prehensile. Adapted for grasping by curling around, e.g. tails of ringtail possums, pygmy-possums etc.

primates. Group of mammals which includes tarsiers, monkeys, apes and humans.

radioactive. Emitting radiation as atomic nuclei within the substance break down.

rodents. Group of gnawing animals, including mice and rats.

scavenger. Animal which feeds on dead animal material it has not killed, e.g. Tasmanian Devil.

silica. A very hard chemical compound. Sand is an example.

syndactylous. Having the second and third toes of the hindfoot joined to the nails. Condition typical of macropods and bandicoots, where conjoined toes are used for grooming.

tarsier. Small, large-eyed, tree-dwelling primate.

torpor. State of inactivity, usually brought about by cold. The animal's metabolic rate slows and it uses less food reserves.

toxic. Poisonous.

tragus. Fleshy flap on the front of the external ear; in microbats the tragus assists with echolocation.

ultrasound. Extremely high-pitched sounds.

venom. Poison produced by an animal.

vertebrates. Animals with backbones. Includes fish, amphibians, reptiles, birds, mammals.

volplane. Glide through air. Mammals such as gliders volplane on flexible membranes.

Map

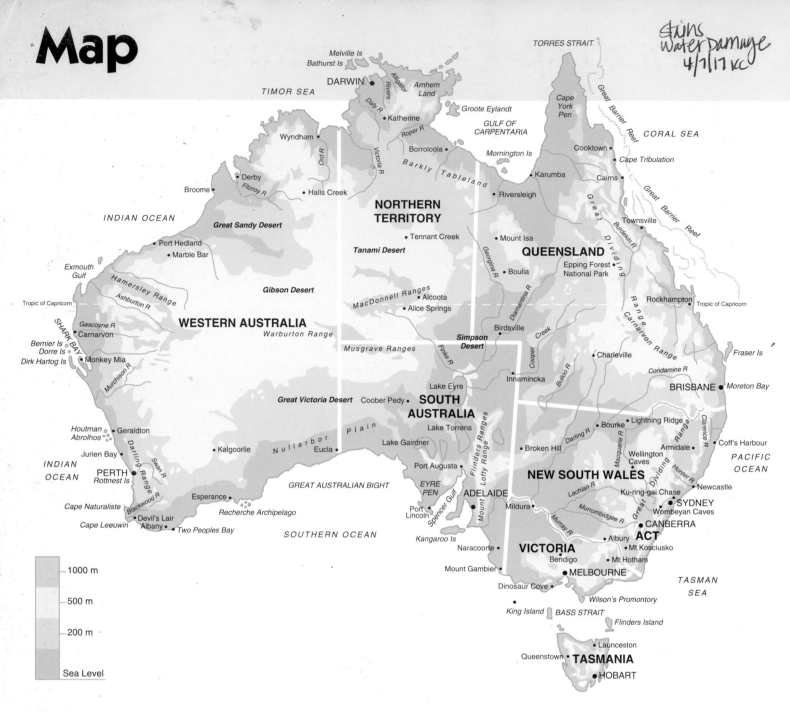

(handwritten annotation top right: "stains / water damage 4/7/17 KC")

Map scale:
- 1000 m
- 500 m
- 200 m
- Sea Level

RECOMMENDED FURTHER READING

BRECKWOLDT, R. 1988. *The Dingo: A Very Elegant Animal*. Angus & Robertson, Sydney.

CRONIN, L. 1991. *Key Guide to Australian Mammals*. Reed Books, Sydney.

CRONIN, L. 1987. *Koala: Australia's Endearing Marsupial*. Leonard Cronin/Reed Books, Sydney.

DAWSON, T. ed. *Australian National History Series* (*Echidnas, Platypus, Koala, Wombat, Dingo etc*). University of New South Wales Press, Sydney.

MUSEUMS OF VARIOUS STATES: Any publications on mammals, by various authors.

STRAHAN, R. ed. 1988. *The Australian Museum Complete Book of Australian Mammals*. Cornstalk Publishing, Sydney. (Revised 1995 as *The Mammals of Australia*. Reed Books, Sydney.)

STRAHAN, R. ed. 1992. *The Australian Museum Encyclopedia of Australian Animals: Mammals*. Angus & Robertson, Sydney.

PHOTOGRAPHY: Steve Parish (uncredited photographs) and Australia's finest wildlife photographers: Stanley Breeden; M & I Morcombe; Ian Morris; Queensland Museum; Mark Simmons; Peter Slater; Lochman Transparencies photographers: Jiri Lochman, Marie Lochman, Wade Hughes, Peter Marsack, Geoff Taylor, as credited.

ACKNOWLEDGEMENTS: The author thanks Bernard Cook, Allan Fox and Ian Morris for their helpful comments on the text.

First published in Australia by Steve Parish Publishing Pty Ltd
PO Box 1058, Archerfield BC, Queensland 4108 Australia
www.steveparish.com.au
© Copyright Steve Parish Publishing Pty Ltd
ISBN 1-875932-32-1

Series designed by Leanne Nobilio, SPP
Cover designed by Leanne Staff, SPP
Printed in Singapore